JUSTICE FOR ELLA

A STORY THAT NEEDED TO BE TOLD

PAM JOHNSON

iUniverse LLC
Bloomington

JUSTICE FOR ELLA
A STORY THAT NEEDED TO BE TOLD

iUniverse books may be ordered through booksellers or by contacting:

iUniverse LLC
1663 Liberty Drive
Bloomington, IN 47403
www.iuniverse.com
1-800-Authors (1-800-288-4677)

Because of the dynamic nature of the Internet, any web addresses or links contained in this book may have changed since publication and may no longer be valid. The views expressed in this work are solely those of the author and do not necessarily reflect the views of the publisher, and the publisher hereby disclaims any responsibility for them.

ISBN: 978-1-4917-3043-0 (sc)
ISBN: 978-1-4917-3044-7 (hc)
ISBN: 978-1-4917-3045-4 (e)

Library of Congress Control Number: 2014907311

Printed in the United States of America.

iUniverse rev. date: 5/1/2014

For
Ella Gaston and Jewell McMahan
and all the other brave foot soldiers in the
struggle for civil rights in Mississippi

CONTENTS

Acknowledgments ix

Prologue xiii

Justice for Ella 1

Ella's Story 4

Jewell's Story 31

The Incident 61

The Trial 126

Ella Gaston v. State of Mississippi 173

Epilogue 199

Author's Notes 213

Selected Resources 231

Appendix – The Decision 235

ACKNOWLEDGMENTS

This book is possible because Jewell McMahan decided the story needed to be told. I am grateful to "Mrs. Mac" and her sons, Mike and Lynn, for giving me the opportunity to put it all on paper. I especially appreciate their never-ending and cheerful patience. I am also grateful to the folks who work with Mrs. Mac and were kind, welcoming, and helpful to me when I invaded their spaces.

I am very thankful to the daughters of Ella and Nelse Gaston, Voncile Burkes and Ima Jean Hill, both of whom were exuberant encouragers and willing to share their memories, documents, and photographs. It was their input that provided the personae of their parents in this telling.

Equally important cheerleaders were my always supportive husband, Bill; our children, Abe and Kasey and Kasey's husband, Lee Woods. My extended family also put up with missed or delayed visits, long stretches of Internet silence, and frenetic phone calls during the writing process. Each and every one of them offered me encouragement and a constant refrain of confidence. I needed every ounce of it.

To the readers who bravely slogged through the various versions of the book—Bill Johnson, Juanise Ableson Stockdale, Margaret Ellis, Dierdre Payne, Emma Gardner, Joyce Buffington Crumley, Kate Jacobson Dutro, Lance and Beth Stevens, Francine Luckett, Norman and Marlane Chronister, Kay McNair Johnson, Ayres Haxton, Kim

LeDuff, Fred and Sandy Middleton, John and Dorothy Hawkins, Tony DiFatta, Voncile Burkett, Jean Hill, Lynn McMahan, and Mike McMahan (at least five times)—your work made this book so much better.

The folks over at the University Press of Mississippi also helped improve the story. I thank Craig Gill, Walter Biggins, and the unnamed readers for their wisdom and guidance as I worked through the best way to tell the story of Ella and Jewell.

Many others who helped me are mentioned in the text of the book, but in the interest of not leaving anyone out, I thank *Macon Beacon* publisher Scott Boyd; Forrest County Agricultural High School secretary Linda Ainsworth; Shuqualak Mayor Velma Jenkins; Macon Mayor Bob Boykin; Noxubee County Chancery Clerk Mary Shelton; Noxubee County Circuit Clerk Carl Mickens; State Representative Reecy Dickson; Noxubee Democratic Party Chair Ike Brown; State National Association for the Advancement of Colored People (NAACP) President Derrick Johnson; the librarians at the Noxubee County Library, the Hattiesburg Library, and the Mississippi Department of Archives and History; former Hinds deputy Steven Pickett and former sheriff Malcolm McMillan; Micah Dutro; Willie Ruth Twilley Jones, Phynes Williams of the Noxubee County Sheriff's Office; and Christine L. Brown of the City of Hattiesburg.

Paula Johnston, Paula Pierce, Beth Colbert, Pam Shaw, Donna Echols, Dorothy Triplett, Judy Clark, Leslie Scott, Vicki Slater, Sherra Hillman Lane, Cindy Mitchell, Lydia Quarles, Gale Walker, Gloria Williamson, and Lynette Keeton provided the all-important girlfriend safety net, and I thank them.

Because this may be my only chance to say it, I also want to thank my high school English teachers Carolyn Smith and Nancy Kay Sullivan Wessman, who taught me how to put organized thoughts on paper; Sylvia Flynt, who taught me how to type them; and Nell Calhoun, who taught me how to publish them. To Betty and Tom Dickson, who gave me my first bylines as a reporter in Magee; the Arrington and Goff families of Collins, who turned me loose with their newspapers; and Bobby Jacobs, who let me publish his magazine, I say thank you for turning me into a real writer.

Last, I've hardly taken a professional step, including this one, during the past twenty years without the encouraging, exacting, and diligent support of Jere Nash, to whom I am exceedingly grateful.

PROLOGUE

My friend Mike McMahan told me this story one summer day in the offhand way of Southern men who tell great tales as standard conversation.

It was his family's story, repeated at the dinner table over the years, but only recently allowed to be aired in public, he said. His mother had always been afraid she'd be arrested if she told anyone about how she and her friend had conspired to foil a gang of white power brokers during the early days of the open civil rights struggle in Mississippi. It was a dangerous time then, and the threat of retribution had pounded heavy in her heart for fifty years.

Then in 2010, Jewell McMahan decreed that her friend's children needed to know what had happened to their mother. So Mike was charged with the task of telling the grown children of Ella Brookshire Gaston the story of how their valiant mother and his had together hatched a plot that confounded some of the most adept racists in the state's history.

Ella's daughters, Jean and Voncile, were shocked and hurt to learn what had happened to their mother, whose motto, even unto her dying day, was, "It's nice to be nice." They were with their parents on the day of "the incident," but neither their poised mother nor their stoic father had ever elaborated on its aftermath. Indeed, the daughters had no idea that their parents, along with their friends

Jewell and Bryce McMahan, had faced down one of the most reviled segregationist sheriffs in Mississippi–and won.

That story forms the basis of this book–a tale about two courageous women, one black and the other white, whose friendship and determination beat the lily-white justice system of Mississippi in 1960. Their caring relationship and the bonds of trust between them enabled the two to overcome what most would have thought an impossible challenge. And, they kept it a virtual secret for five decades.

I was honored with the task of writing it all down, with the caveat accepted that I am a storyteller and not a historian. My writing background is as a journalist and publicist. As an English teacher, I provided my students with plenty of opportunities to do research papers but never pretended that research was my own strong point.

So I viewed my job to be bringing to life the protagonists and the men who supported and loved them, placing this tale into the context of Mississippi's miserable racial history as it affected the period in which the story took place, and weaving a narrative that would both entertain and inform.

All of the principals are deceased except for Jewell, and so I relied upon additional interviews of other people who knew the players to help flesh out their characters along with whatever historical documents may have been available.

There are mentions of the various components of Mississippi's history that affected the times in which the McMahans and Gastons found themselves–some of them widely known, some of them not so much, some recent, some very old. Nevertheless, a complete telling of this tale would not be possible without defining the tableau upon which the story played out.

Most of us in Mississippi are scaldingly aware of why our state owns the tarnished reputation it bears in matters of race. And, many of us are trying mightily to overcome the burdens that awful reputation imposes. Sometimes we still feel we are swimming upstream against a torrent of the old ideas, customs, and ways barreling toward us like a rush of cold runoff from the top of a melting mountain.

To me, the saga was a sublime example of civil rights struggles that took place across Mississippi apart from the headline-grabbing racist horrors that were riveting the rest of midcentury America. Mike believed it to be a story that needed to be written—not only for Jewell McMahan and Ella Gaston but also for the other black and white foot soldiers in the civil rights movement who battled against seemingly insurmountable meanness to rise above and claim their mutual humanity as more important than social structure.

We both believed our players in the state's civil rights struggles were just a handful of the hundreds of other valiant unknowns whose stories of courage, friendship, and heroism remain today only as tales around family dinner tables. Hopefully, this telling would inspire others to come forward with their own stories.

We hoped the effort would at least offer readers with preconceived notions the idea that, in 1959, all white people in Mississippi were not abject racists. We wanted readers to understand that black people countered racially motivated outrage by fighting back with whatever means were available to them.

While most everything in this book is fact, minor things have been rearranged, names have been changed, and I've filled in the blanks on some settings and characters to help drive the plot—although I must say that the story practically told itself.

By the time I arrived for my first meeting with Jewell, I had come to know there was an entire repertoire of Jewell Clark McMahan stories describing a larger-than-life character.

At ninety-one years old, Jewell retained all of the spitfire that had made her into a legend around Hattiesburg, Mississippi, and on the national nursing home stage. On this late summer morning, she was holding court in the breakfast room of her bright yellow kitchen. I was there to record the amazing story in which she was a primary player and to write it down because it needed to be told.

With a perfectly coiffed head of bright red hair, freshly applied black eyelashes, and a newly done French manicure, she sat down, smoothed her white damask tablecloth, and prepared to finally tell the tale of how the paths and threads of her life had led her here, to this day, September 2, 2010, where she finally felt free to tell the story of *Ella Gaston v. State of Mississippi* without fear.

And, Jewell's intent was to tell it all—for herself and for her departed friend Ella.

JUSTICE FOR ELLA

Driving While Black

Shuqualak, Mississippi–February 22, 1959, 3:00 p.m.

"Nelse! What's wrong?" Ella whispered.

He'd been slowing down and watching the rearview mirror. She could see blinking red lights reflecting off the dashboard.

"I don't know," Nelse said, carefully pulling his shiny green and white Ford Fairlane over to the shoulder. Their four children in back sat quiet as baby birds in a disturbed nest.

Within seconds, the Gaston family found themselves surrounded by white men with badges, guns, nightsticks, and nasty attitudes.

Nelse rolled down his window far enough to hear one of them yell, "Get out, nigger!"

As soon as Nelse's feet hit the ground, the officer dragged him to the back of the car, out of his family's sight.

"Put your hands up!" they could hear the officer shouting. "I said put your hands up, nigger!"

The distinctive sound of fist on flesh came next, and the car heaved as Nelse fell against it. He was on the ground, and all four officers were scrambling against gravel on asphalt to get a lick in. The family could hear their grunts and curses.

"Stop it! Quit!" a white man's voice shouted, and the thudding commotion ceased.

Pulled to his feet, scraped and bleeding, Nelse was handcuffed behind his back. He was weaving a little where he stood, and a welt on his forehead stuck out like a hen egg.

"What's in the trunk, nigger?"

"Nothing."

"Aw, you gonna lie now?"

"There's nothing in there, man."

"Well, we're fixin' to find out."

"Wait, man! Wait! Get the key out of the ignition! Don't tear up my car, man!"

It was too late.

The hacking had already started as a broad-shouldered officer tore off the Continental Kit with a tire iron and jimmied open the trunk for a look inside.

"You were right, nigger. Nothing. How 'bout that?"

The passengers could hear chuckling and one or two loud guffaws.

"Be still, children," Ella ordered.

She took a deep breath, straightened her shoulders, and stepped out of the car.

"What's wrong? Why are you doing this to my husband?"

"Shut up, nigger," a skinny officer said, grabbing her by the arm.

"Come on over here, and we'll see what kind of trouble you're in, gal."

He spun her around and slammed her head and face into the car while he pressed against her, running his hands along the length of her body and eventually slapping a set of handcuffs on her slim wrists.

The skinny one checked her all over one more time. Her blouse had lost a button by the time he was done.

Ella was silent. So was Nelse as he watched.

"Let's get them outta here," a uniformed one muttered.

As the couple was shoved into the back of the patrol car, Ella looked over her shoulder and shouted to her children, "Call Hermene! Tell her to call Mrs. Mac!"

Then they were gone—red lights flashing, tires spinning, and sirens blaring. Only the men in tan uniforms and the four children in the backseat of the Ford Fairlane were left on the road in front of the big white house that belonged to Pete Flora.

After a twenty-minute ride up Highway 45, the patrol car whipped into the graveled back parking lot of the Noxubee County jail, across the street from the courthouse.

The jail, though lovely from the outside, was rotten on the inside. This Nelse knew. He'd been told tales of what happened inside those beautiful brick walls all his life. It wasn't good for anybody, but it was awful for black men and rumored to be worse than that for black women.

He knew there was an eyelet in the tin ceiling in the middle of the cell block where the hangman's noose was supposed to go. He knew that sometimes there was an empty noose just hanging there, glowering. He knew that sometimes people went inside and came out beaten up or worse. He knew this was one place neither he nor his wife needed to be.

Soon enough, they were booked in.

Ella never told anyone exactly what she endured that night. But whatever it was caused her and her friend Jewell McMahan to make a solemn pledge that Ella would never spend another night in jail. Never. Never again. No matter the cost and no matter what they had to do to prevent it.

ELLA'S STORY

Noxubee

Up in the eastern red dirt part of Mississippi, midcentury Noxubee County rested secure in its reputation as a place where black Mississippians dared not threaten the menacing and blustering societal structure that kept them "in their places."

A predominantly agricultural society that relied upon enslavement of people of African descent had left its remnants in a stark and vast divide between an elite white upper class served by a merchant and service industry-dominated white middle class and a black class with few acknowledged rights, scant wealth, insufficient educational opportunity, and little hope for change.

The system of exclusion and oppression pervading living arrangements of about 70 percent of the county's occupants hadn't been achieved overnight. As far back as the hopeful days of Reconstruction when black new citizens were actually participating in their government, the county christened "Stinking Water" by its native residents was making a name for itself in terms of racial terrorism—all the way to the halls of Congress.

As for the original nonwhite inhabitants of the area, they were essentially gone a generation before the first shot was fired at Fort Sumter.

In September 1830, colorful Choctaw chieftain Mushulatubbee (Choctaw for "determined to kill") signed the Treaty of Dancing Rabbit Creek and ceded eleven million acres of ancestral lands to the United States government in exchange for land in Oklahoma and Arkansas. In so doing, he threw his tribe's homeland wide open to an influx of urgently pioneering white farmers, most with Scotch-Irish pedigrees, and their entourage of dark brown laborers.

In effect, Mushulatubbee's decision to participate in his tribe's three-year "removal" to Oklahoma took away one large nonwhite group from the Noxubee countryside and made way for another group, which was enslaved.

Noxubee County was organized as a county of seven hundred square miles on December 23, 1833, along with several other political subdivisions of the ceded Choctaw lands. Noxubee sidled up to Alabama to the east, bore a significant ridge running southeast to northwest that supported bountiful hardwood and pine forests to its west, and overlooked flat river plains to the east. The county seemed perfectly formed to support the plantation lifestyle of its new white settlers.

Established in 1836 as the county seat, Macon was a bustling hub of commerce, catering to its wealthy inhabitants. Town matrons orchestrated plenty of high-society occasions to rival legendary Southern seats of wealth on parade, like Charleston, Richmond, and Natchez. Macon boasted a fine courthouse, a secure jailhouse, an impressive bank building, and a variety of newspapers turning out news for at least a couple of decades by the time "The War" broke out in 1861.

Planters with thousands of acres of growing land and hundreds of slaves to manage them built large and impressive homes in Macon to shield their families from the realities of the system supporting them. Brooksville and Shuqualak had been incorporated a scant few years before war was declared, but the genteel ways of the county seat were replicated in the smaller towns just as well.

Before the "War for Southern Independence," the privileged children of the Noxubee ruling class had been privately schooled in much-sought-after institutions within the county, such as the Calhoun Institute, a private school for girls whose classic architecture rivaled that of Windsor down near Port Gibson, and the Summerville Institute for Boys. On the day Mississippi seceded from the Union, the *Macon Beacon* carried an advertisement for the Calhoun Institute wherein headmaster W. R. Poindexter extolled his school as "a limited select school for young ladies." Instruction was provided by men, and the modern languages were taught by European professors. Great emphasis was placed upon the playing of musical instruments by the students. The Summerville Institute was the only secondary school to continue operation in Mississippi during the later days of the war.

Isolated from major thoroughfares of battle, Macon enjoyed a relatively unscathed existence during the bloody turbulence that ravaged the rest of the state. So secure was Macon's sanctuary, Mississippi's state government fled from brief stopovers in Columbus and Meridian to the shelter of the Calhoun Institute in 1863 after Jackson's first fall. The town hosted a session of the legislature and provided residences for Mississippi government officials, including the state's twenty-fourth governor, Charles Clark, who took up domicile at John Morgan's house just east of town. Indeed, Macon was at the apex of prominence in the Magnolia State even as Confederate president Jefferson Davis, a Mississippian, was presiding over the dissolving Confederacy from his perch in Richmond, Virginia.

On May 6, 1865, the same day that Confederate general Richard Taylor surrendered to Union general Canby over in Meridian, Governor Clark, himself a seriously wounded rebel veteran, decided to convene the legislature in special session back in Jackson to determine the most advantageous way to surrender the state government. He departed Macon for the capital. Unsurprisingly, occupying Union forces in Jackson exercised the privilege of deciding the appropriate method of surrender. It was succinct: disband or be arrested. Legislators had barely made it into the capital city for the May 18 session when they turned around and fled to what was left of their homes, rather than face arrest. The governor himself was formally removed from office on May 22 and hauled off to Fort Pulaski in Georgia for a time in federal custody. Meanwhile, Union commanders were comfortably ensconced at the Governor's Mansion on Capitol Street.

By this time, a demolished Jackson had been the scene of at least five hard-fought takeovers by Yankee troops. For some white residents of Mississippi, the humiliation of watching their state government leaders running through the countryside while their proud capital was overrun by the looting, burning enemy time after time engendered a lasting hatred of anything federal, particularly when the national government told them what to do. Exacerbated by the postwar federal insistence on recognition of freedmen as equal citizens under the law, the entrenched hatred toward the victors never left the hearts of some diehard rebels.

Embittered survivors taught those lessons to following generations well into the twentieth century.

Despite the war's outcome, Macon hardly changed. For its white citizenry, who had lived through the degradation of defeat without much bloodshed in their own backyards, the bitter determination to maintain the "Southern Way of Life" remained a motivating cause for over a hundred years.

The fact that hundreds of thousands of people had given their lives to change how black people were able to lead theirs in the

South seemed an unnecessary waste of human blood. At least it appeared so in Noxubee County. Other than the actuality that nobody held a title of ownership on their persons, most freed people's lives remained largely embroiled in hard labor and servitude to the familiar moneyed and landed white gentry of their past.

Just because black people had few opportunities to extract themselves from their impoverished conditions didn't for one minute mean they weren't still perceived as threats to their nervous white neighbors. And so, Noxubee County began to make a name for itself as a hotbed and a haven for the Ku Klux Klan, the notorious organization established to intimidate newly freed black people from attempting to exercise their basic rights as American citizens.

The May 14, 1870, *Macon Beacon* carried the following editorial commentary entitled "KU-KLUX":

> It is generally believed in the North that a widespread organization exists in our midst, whose object is, by acts of lawless violence, to thwart the restoration of law and order, and make victims of all who are inimical to their proceedings. The frequency of these secret mobs, for such they are, has given color to that supposition, and legislation has been busy to counteract the evil tendencies of such associations. The existence of a Ku-Klux society, as understood there, we believe, is a myth, and this outbreak of disconnected bands, in all parts of the country, can be traced to no fountainhead, but seems to be the offspring of local causes wherever a few turbulent spirits imagine they must take the law into their hands and inflict vengeance on all who cross their path. This spirit is much to be

deprecated, and ought to be suppressed, but we fear legislation will but aggravate the evil. It rests with the law-abiding citizens to frown down the violent Klans, who veil with secrecy the most revolting crimes, and stain a whole people with the guilt and darkness of their transactions. What they call executing the law is simply assassination, and often aggravated, too, by orgies from which an inquisition would shrink with horror. The good they do is simply nothing, the harm is incalculable. For men to make a common property of their prejudices and strike its objects in the dark is monstrous. When law and order is endeavoring to crystallize itself into shape, to obstruct it because it acts slowly, is nil [wort]hy of good citizens. These midnight banditti are doing more to thwart the peace and prosperity of our country than a wise legislation of years could counteract. Our people should persistently endeavor to remove these foul ulcers that now and then break out where bad blood exists, and apply remedies that will finally restore these diseased spots to healthy action. It can be done calmly, soothingly, but it must be done firmly. It should be made disreputable to aid or countenance such outrages, and the very perpetrators will then pause and look back with horror on the deeds of darkness which they have blindly committed.

One year later, on May 13, 1871, the *Beacon* carried the following excerpt of a speech that former Union general William T. Sherman gave at Vicksburg, as reported by the *Vicksburg Herald*: "I probably have as good means of information as most persons in regard to what is called the Ku-Klux, and am perfectly satisfied that the thing is greatly over estimated; and if the Ku-Klux bills were kept out of Congress, and the army kept at their legitimate duties, there are enough good and true men in all southern States to put down all Ku-Klux or other bands of marauders."

Despite the general's unusual, yet hopeful, outlook, reports of vicious mistreatment of blacks in the South by marauding thugs in costume created such a stir in Washington that Congress held a hearing on the subject that year. The Joint Select Committee to Inquire into the Condition of Affairs in the Late Insurrectionary States convened with the innocuous duty of merely checking into how the Southern states were faring during Reconstruction but in fact devoted much of its time to gaining sworn testimony about the activities of the Ku-Kluxers.

Congress had passed the Ku Klux Klan Act of 1871 in April, which made nightriders actual criminals, not just in deed, but also on the books.

In July, John R. Taliaferro, a Noxubee resident originally from Virginia, was one of fifty-two witnesses summoned to the nation's capital to testify before the congressional panel investigating reports of outrages against former slaves and their sympathizers. Taliaferro testified that there had been from fifteen to twenty murders within the previous nine months. He talked about murders of black men he was personally aware of, described a beating he had witnessed, and explained to the panel how the preferred method "to straighten out the niggers" was to strip them to the skin and beat them. Men, women, and children alike received this treatment. He personally knew of women of African descent who had been pulled from homes where they lived with white men and stripped and beaten as a lesson against miscegenation. There was hardly any mention made as to whether or not their white male lovers protested or in any way attempted to stop the attacks, but Taliaferro confirmed that none of the men were harmed during the raids.

Taliaferro also provided details of loose Klan organizations and their manner of "secret" communications with salutes like "Hail" and "Mount Nebo." Importantly, he revealed two main motives for targeting individual blacks: 1) they were renting land coveted by white would-be farmers, or 2) they were voting for Republicans. He also mentioned former Confederate general Nathan Bedford Forrest, as the generally recognized organizer of the Klan. His railroad-building operation was headquartered just north of Macon in Columbus at the time.

For his testimony, Taliaferro was characterized as a drunkard, liar, murderer, and mule thief by his neighbor, insurance agent Charles Baskerville, during his own sworn deposition to the committee.

When a congressional subcommittee was dispatched from Washington to Mississippi in November 1871 to get some on-the-ground information, Macon was the first place they went. In all, they entertained testimony from ten whites and six blacks while there. Witnesses stated that in the previous year, acts of "whippings" of both "colored" and white people were documented. Of those murdered, twelve were colored and two were white. The earlier reports of terrors in Noxubee County appeared to have been alarmingly accurate.

For his part, Governor Ridgley C. Powers, himself a Noxubee County cotton planter and a pragmatic Republican, blamed all the commotion on sneaky wrongdoers who had come into Noxubee County from Alabama.

The Klan Act effectively dismantled the loosely organized bands, and it wasn't until the 1920s that klaverns began to make recognizable noises again. A group called Women of the Ku Klux Klan went so far as to register themselves with the Mississippi Secretary of State's Office in 1924.

Some undoubtedly suspected when the Klan raised its hooded head again in Mississippi that Noxubee County was a place it would most certainly find succor. The Klan was notoriously right at home in the not-so-distant counties of Neshoba and Lauderdale, as later evidenced in the horrible civil rights murder cases of the 1960s. But if the Klan was indeed roaming the roads of Noxubee County by the 1950s, no sheets, hoods, or mysterious greetings were necessary. All appeared to be well in hand for the white power structure.

In most of twentieth-century Noxubee County, black people were kept from voting; they were eliminated from juries (assuming they received summonses); they couldn't publicly befriend white people of their own gender, much less the opposite; and they couldn't stand on the same sidewalk or eat at the same table as white people. They entered and exited all public buildings and almost all businesses through the back doors. They sat in the balcony of the Dreamland, Noxubee County's only movie theater. They were barred from worshipping in the white churches, even those with slave galleries overlooking their sanctuaries where the races had once worshipped under the same roof. And, black people in Noxubee County were still occasionally murdered with impunity.

One of the most infamous tales of unpunished racial violence is the story of Macon businessman Lionel Traner and the bridge. In the early 1950s, Ms. Estelle Cantrell, a black domestic worker who was said to be highly regarded by the white folks in the Piney Woods and Brooksville areas of the county, was riding into Macon with her son behind the wheel of their car. As they approached the one-lane bridge over a small creek on what is now known as the Macon-Lynn Creek Road, the two noticed a car coming toward them. It was driven by Traner. The Cantrells kept going and proceeded on toward town, forcing Traner and his passenger to wait. The young driver had unknowingly violated the "step aside" rule in force in all matters of travel–by foot, wagon, or car–in Noxubee County, whereby black travelers were required to stand down and allow whites to pass. Traner allegedly turned his car around and chased the Cantrells, eventually running them off the road at the feed mill in Macon. Traner, it is said, then jumped out of his car, went to the driver's open window, and shot the young Cantrell dead. Ms. Cantrell caught her son's slumping body in her arms as he died. Traner got back in his car, turned around, and headed back out across the bridge, only a little late to his original appointment. When questioned, Traner claimed self-defense. He was never prosecuted despite two eyewitnesses having been on the scene. Such was racial justice in midcentury Noxubee County.

Dorroh Hill Road

"Durr Hill," as the locals say, is an insulated stretch of gravel road running for about a mile and a half southwest of Shuqualak. It's not very easy to find. Even today, a person has to be going there on purpose because it's not on the way to or from anything else.

The road was named for the Dorroh family of early white Noxubee settlers whose progeny dominated much of the county's government in the decades covering the turn of the twentieth century. Z. T. (Zachary Taylor) Dorroh, a Confederate veteran who served under General Forrest, was the county's sheriff and chancery clerk for a number of terms. His son Iva Lamar was elected to the Mississippi State House while simultaneously serving his father as a deputy circuit clerk. Another son, Clinton Edwards Dorroh, served in the state senate. In the 1917 centennial edition of the state's *Official and Statistical Register*, Dorroh's lush profile as written by historian Dunbar Rowland crowed that Dorroh was "of Welsh blood," "one of the purest and oldest races that inhabit the British Isles." Such things seemed important to note at the time.

While the African American adults of Noxubee County likely bowed their heads and prayed for a final deliverance from the familiar oppression that plagued their ancestors, the black children of Dorroh Hill Road managed to live an almost idyllic life during the early part of the twentieth century.

Everything a child needed was contained in that one little stretch of civilization—plenty of playmates, farm animals, well water, gardens, and long, open fields. Shiloh Baptist Church was visible to most everybody, and so was the one-room school sheltered in the M. B. church down the road.

Most Dorroh Hill fathers farmed their own few acres of land, and some worked odd jobs for white people in town or big farms out in the county. Mothers who worked outside of their homes drew wages as domestic help in white people's houses commanding the six-square-block area of Shuqualak proper. Some Dorroh Hill residents picked cotton on the nearby plantations in the time-honored tradition of backbreaking labor begun in the region a hundred years previously by their enslaved relatives.

Racial integration was a foreign idea to most people in Noxubee County in the early part of the twentieth century, and certainly for the youngest inhabitants of the Dorroh Hill community, who endured little regular contact with whites. For the children, there just wasn't much reason to think about how life was conducted outside of their close-knit community. When they ventured out of it, rules of separation were strictly enforced by whites who were determined to maintain control in a society in which they themselves were a decided minority. Census results show that whites were about 30 percent of the population in 1920.

There was one thing about segregation—unless you were just forced out into the white world, a black person could build a whole, pleasant life apart from the dangerous and demeaning realities of apartheid as practiced in the American South.

Places like Beale Street in Memphis and Farish Street in Jackson thrived as shielded microeconomies where, for at least some of the time, peace-loving and upright citizens of African descent could celebrate the joys of living without fear or degradation. In a smaller and certainly less musical extent, the same could be said for Dorroh Hill.

At Dorroh Hill, a person was free to be free.

Little Ella

Ella Cornelia Brookshire was the daughter of "Professor" Edgar and Jesse Brookshire, both educators. Born prematurely on February 18, 1913, she was the last of their five children. Jesse, thirty-seven, died from a hemorrhage when her baby was eight days old. Edgar took the two-pound newborn to the home of his sister Ella Carter on Dorroh Hill Road for help.

His sister refused. She already had one child too many, she protested, referring to her only child, Cleo.

"Please just keep her 'til she dies," Edgar begged, handing over the mewling baby on a pillow. "She probably won't live more than a day or two. I just can't do it." He had four other children to manage, and his teaching job was at Running Water School, miles from Shuqualak. Plus, he had his wife to bury.

Reluctantly, and with the assumption that the job would only last for a day or two, Aunt Ella accepted the duty to watch over the infant until she passed. Without warning, the aunt's maternal instincts triumphed, and Ella Carter took on the care and feeding of her niece as a fierce challenge to Death. Two days passed, then a week, then a month, and eventually the baby began to thrive. Her auntie may have been proud of herself, but she was not an enthusiastic caregiver. Aunt Ella named her charge after herself and resigned to do the best she could with her. At least the baby would make for an extra pair of hands.

Aunt Ella lived in a nice frame house just south of the Slaughter family cemetery on Dorroh Hill Road. The house was remarkable in that its clapboard siding was painted white, as opposed to the weathered gray of most of its neighbors. White hand-stitched curtains fluttered from windows flanked with green shutters. There was even a swing on the home's wide front porch.

So Little Ella grew up in a quintessential country home where she learned the fine arts of homemaking from her aunt. By the time she left to start her own home, Little Ella was an accomplished seamstress and an unrivaled cook, her talents in the kitchen still dominating conversations about her years after her death.

The tutelage, however, was harsh. Little Ella was saddled with chores and often assigned duty for the white ladies in town who hired her aunt to maintain their laundry. Once on a particularly icy Monday, ten-year-old Ella was walking the two miles into Shuqualak, carrying a bundle of laundry, when her foot slipped on the rickety bridge spanning a little stream on the way. She fell between the planks, somehow managing to balance the cleaning above her head with one hand. Ice was everywhere, and she was terrified of the water. Like most of the Dorroh Hill community, she'd never learned to swim. Finally, she flailed into a root and pulled her way back onto the bridge. The clothes never knew the difference. It was a good thing. Little Ella would have suffered a beating if she'd soiled them.

The child bore the guilt of her mother's death. Every time Professor Brookshire saw his youngest daughter, she reminded him of the wife he had lost. Consequently, he took very little time for the daughter on Dorroh Hill Road; he kept himself busy raising the older four children. As a result, the opportunity to enjoy being a sister to her siblings was rarely available to the baby of the family.

Little Ella said she found the Lord while working in cotton fields at the age of sixteen, and, in the way of the community culture, she absorbed teachings of the church into her everyday existence, reading and memorizing Bible verses and practicing the Fruits of the Spirit in her dealings with others. In the tidy sanctuary of Shiloh Baptist Church, Ella's lilting voice sang comforting hymns of the faith and familiar spirituals of those who had gone before. Church was the central activity of her life, a safe haven, and it would continue to be so for as long as she lived.

Unlike her playmates, Little Ella never graduated from the one-room school just down the road, nor did she venture over to Reed School, the "colored" high school at Shuqualak, to complete her studies. Her work under Aunt Ella's strict chore enforcement interfered with regular school attendance. That didn't stop her from reading everything she could find, and she wished longingly to join her friends in the adventures of schooling. But the opportunity slipped away in the day-to-day drudgery of laundry, house cleaning, and fieldwork.

Ella determined that if the Lord blessed her with children, she would see to it that each one would go to school and experience the joys of a childhood she never knew. They would play.

In the late 1920s and early 1930s, the concept of "separate but equal" educational opportunities had not gelled in Noxubee County.

The "separate" part was figured out pretty well, but as for the "equal" part, the "colored" schools were mostly in churches or abandoned farm outbuildings. They were leaky and drafty, textbooks were old and worn, and teachers were overwhelmed by the number of students and courses assigned to their instruction. Most of the time, one or two teachers taught the entire assemblage in one space, covering the grades one by one as they worked the room, and the children completed their lessons on their own. Somehow, education took place, but little was said about important blacks who contributed to the historical, literary, scientific, and political advancements of the United States of America. It would take the Freedom Schools of 1964 to ensure that those courses were taught to the black children of Mississippi, and even then, they were not taught in Noxubee County.

Occasionally, the *Macon Beacon* posted a paragraph or two about the "colored" school's athletic accomplishments, but not much else was reported about 70 percent of the county's population except to name "the coloreds" who were admitted to the local hospital.

When the Colored Fair came to Macon, though, that was a different story. Established in 1922, the event was announced in a two-page spread by 1939. In addition to proclaiming every kind of fair food and entertainment available at most any county fair of the day, the Colored Fair also boasted a vast array of exhibits sure to be significant to Noxubee's black women, who were often housekeepers for white people. The Thrift Exhibit, which showcased clothing items made from "feed, flour, and other bags," offered opportunities for those who were talented with the needle to show off their quilts, children's dresses, and hair combing jackets. The Laundry Exhibit featured items of particular importance to people working as domestics–best lye soap white; best lye soap plain; best-laundered man's shirt; best-laundered fancy dress in voile, organdie, or Swiss;

and, unsurprisingly, best-laundered housedress. The families of Dorroh Hill Road looked forward to the fair every year.

She was capable, kind, and determined, but the most significant thing about Ella Brookshire was something she didn't really notice much. Others did that for her. She was simply beautiful. With creamy, caramel skin and a delicate, long neck, Ella carried herself regally on a demure frame. Her hair was smooth and thick, and she wore it to her shoulders in the classic pageboy style. With her high cheekbones, astonishingly bright smile, and carriage of a queen, Ella was the catch of the community.

Just down the road in a three-room gray farmhouse belonging to Cap Gaston, a young man of the family was paying close attention to his striking neighbor. John Nelse Gaston was a looker in his own right. He bore the slender, tight build of a natural athlete and presented himself as best he could in the high fashion style of men in places significantly more sophisticated than Dorroh Hill Road.

Yes, one thing people could always count on with Nelse was his impeccable, stylish presentation—that is, except for the fact that he didn't wear a white shirt. In Noxubee County, it was common knowledge in the community that black men weren't allowed to wear white shirts. It made them look too "uppity" according to an edict handed down decades earlier by some unknown white man. The uppity distinction was beaten out of more than one Noxubee County black man over the mistake of wearing a white shirt out in public. So Nelse wore tan or blue, a habit he continued long into his adulthood whenever he ventured back into Noxubee County.

One might say that in this world, there are two types of people: those who maintain their things and those who don't. Nelse Gaston presented the maintenance profile. He shined his shoes, he sharpened the blades, he mowed the lawn every week whether it needed it or not, he swept the roof, he sealed the windows, he oiled the hinges, he tended the garden and livestock, and he lovingly and proudly waxed the car—all rituals marking him as a responsible gentleman and, to some, framing him as excellent husband material.

Apparently, Ella Brookshire thought so.

He asked for her hand, and she accepted. It wasn't as though Ella and Nelse met one day and experienced a whirlwind courtship ending in a lightning-strike wedding ceremony. Theirs was a relationship nurtured by shared childhoods and all the unspoken understandings enjoyed by couples who have grown up together.

They married at the home of his parents in 1932. At-home weddings were the custom of the day; very few African American couples married in church ceremonies in rural Noxubee County. Ella was nineteen years old.

Both Ella and Nelse had been brought up in households valuing decorum and respectability. Ella was quick-witted and entertaining while maintaining a slight air of formality. She developed a way of speaking that transcended her rural background and made outside listeners wonder if she was actually from the Islands. Her intent was to sound cultured and educated, her children said after she was gone. Nelse was quiet in a way that meant everyone listened when he finally spoke. They were kind and respectful to their family members, their elders, and each other. They practiced self-discipline in matters of behavior and finance. The couple complemented each other very nicely.

Newman Quarters

The Gastons made their home with Cousin Cleo, Aunt Ella's daughter. Nelse worked day labor on various farming operations around Shuqualak; Ella reared the children and occasionally worked alongside her kinswomen as a cook or domestic help for the white women in town.

Soon after World War II started, Nelse and Ella decided to move out of the impoverished backwoods of Shuqualak and Mississippi. A leg injury sustained in a horrific car accident had prevented Nelse from going to war, and so the couple set their sights on Florida as the Promised Land.

Nelse headed south for the Sunshine State on a reconnoitering mission, taking a detour by Hattiesburg, where his friends from Noxubee County, George and Billie Hopkins, had settled. Nelse just wanted to pay a friendly visit. As it turned out, that detour changed everything.

When Nelse arrived, George was preparing for an interview at the Hercules Powder Plant over in the Mobile-Bouie Street neighborhood. The Hercules plant was one of Hattiesburg's largest employers and manufactured chemicals from remnants of the pine lumber business and components for various other products, including ammunition. War had swelled its need for employees.

Nelse offered to get out of George's way and head on to Florida, but his friend invited Nelse to come along for the interview. Once they got there, the plant manager looked over both men. He told Nelse he could tell by looking at him that he was a hard worker. He didn't say the same to George. Nelse was hired. George wasn't. (Years later, as her children were growing up, Ella cautioned them in the sternest tones never to take anyone with them on a job interview.)

So with Ella pregnant with Jean, and three other little ones in tow, the Gastons moved their homestead down to Forrest County, to the snug little neighborhood of Newman Quarters in Hattiesburg.

At first, the Gaston family lived in rented property on Davis Street, where Jean was born. Ten years and three children later, Nelse built his family a nice house around the corner on Lee Street featuring indoor plumbing and a kitchen boasting all the modern appliances. He personally selected materials, oversaw construction, and helped build the house–as always, attending to the details. The Gaston children could hardly believe their new status–residents of a brand new home–as they watched their dad and his friends build the house from the ground up. To have indoor plumbing was a luxury.

By this time, Nelse worked for Central Packing Company nearby the Newman Quarters. Although Ella had worked briefly at Camp Shelby during the war, she was now busy making a home for Nelse and their seven children–Hermene, Juanita, Leauvel, Jean, Clifford, Voncile, and Michael.

Much like the Dorroh Hill Road community back home in Noxubee, Lee Street's neighborhood was a destination, not a pass-through. As such, it enabled the kind of close-knit, neighborly ways that offer children the security of a broadly nurturing society.

It was situated in the Leaf River floodplain, unfortunately often true to its designation. Floodwaters plagued residents with insistent periodic incursions into yards, vehicles, and, occasionally, houses. Nevertheless, other than the occasional springtime flood, life was good and safe there.

Newman Quarters was swarming with children. From her kitchen, Ella could hear their voices as they played ball or "hidey seek" or drew off little farms and playhouses in her yard. "Miz Ella" preferred the neighborhood to come to her house, and they did.

Her house was a drop-off point for the yellow school buses ferrying children to and from their segregated schools. As a result, the Gaston yard appeared tramped down and not nearly so well manicured as those of its neighbors. To neighborhood children, it was their perfect, welcoming playground.

Ella had stayed true to her childhood ambition. She'd provided her own children the childhood she'd been denied—they enjoyed the luxury of play.

This was an era and an opportunity for grown-ups to engage in the age-old tradition of tending one another's flocks. The youngsters benefitted from the sure understanding that they were both protected by the neighborhood parents' kindly vigilance and also subject to their stern discipline.

In Newman Quarters, everybody was your mother. You behaved around everybody or you got a spanking. It didn't matter whose mother was administering the punishment, and Miz Ella was a no-nonsense mother. She treated each little one as though he or she were her own. She was strict, but the neighborhood children knew she loved them. And they loved her.

One of the hallmarks of the wisdom she imparted to the children who entered her door was to get an education. "It's the most important thing you can do for yourself," she'd say. "Nobody can take an education from you."

Like Ella's childhood home on Dorroh Hill Road, the Gaston residence in Newman Quarters was white with green shutters. It also had a green roof in the fashion of the 1940s, and its windows were covered with Ella's hand-sewn ruffled curtains. Inside were sparkling linoleum floors and homemade bedspreads.

Ella most often wore dresses she made herself. She also sewed her daughters' clothes. Being a seamstress was not an unusual avocation for the mothers of Newman Quarters. Every season the women would go downtown to the JC Penney store on Pine Street and purchase for a dollar each, four yards of every new fabric. Four yards was plenty enough material to make an outfit, and so the mothers would be able to dress their daughters for a dollar or less.

Not one outfit was made alike; each mother cut her own imaginative patterns from newspaper. Even though the fabrics were the same, the looks that the able seamstresses created were completely different.

Never ones to leave anything for waste, the ladies incorporated the fabric scraps into quilt making. Not only were neighborhood closets full of the same colors and motifs, beds from one house to the next looked awfully familiar. The blend of colors and patterns at every turn helped make for an even more cohesive community.

Mount Bethel Baptist Church anchored the neighborhood's social structure because many of the adults were either working or too busy at home to do much visiting during the week. The church was a red brick building with a baptistery in the back of the sanctuary, a lovely natural oak ceiling, and seats for about 150 congregants. When the music got going and the sound of feet tapping on the wooden floors began to call in rhythm, the congregation knew they were having church.

Both Nelse and Ella were church ushers. Without air-conditioning, the congregants used iconic church fans to relieve the heat. Ella carried one in her gloved hand for another purpose. Whenever she spotted a child who had managed to sneak into service with a wad of gum in his or her mouth, Ella would serenely slide her fan under the offender's chin. With the gum neatly deposited on the fan, the lovely usher would retreat to her place in the back of the sanctuary and quietly look for the next offender. All it took was a look and that fan, and Miz Ella was in complete control of the younger members of the congregation.

During the worship service, older women, the mothers of the church, sat on a reserved bench to the right, and their male counterparts sat on the left. Choir members were seated to the side of the preacher. Ella had a beautiful voice, and she loved to sing the old hymns from the choir loft whenever she wasn't patrolling the aisle with her gum-laden fan.

Like many Southern churches then and now, Mount Bethel occasionally observed a "dinner on the ground," which literally *was* a dinner on the ground. The congregation mothers packed boxes and baskets with enough homemade food to feed their families and everyone else and then spread the fragrant meals out on quilts under trees in the churchyard after service.

It was generally understood that everyone got in line at Ella's box first. They wanted her German chocolate cake and her rolls, especially. And, of course, her fried chicken was a most popular menu item. Using only salt, pepper, and plain flour to dress the chicken parts, Ella arranged them in a certain order in her large black skillet popping with melted Crisco. The smaller pieces went to the outside of the pan; larger pieces like breasts and thighs went in the middle over the flame. Timing was everything with fried chicken, and "hurry" wasn't part of the process.

Ella didn't reserve her cooking talents just for church socials. She cooked enough food at every meal to feed about fifteen people, which could easily be the number standing around in the house at any given mealtime. She always made extra food, and she instructed the children to deliver it to whoever in the neighborhood was sick or couldn't cook for themselves.

Neither seven children nor age had diminished Ella Gaston's great beauty during her time on Lee Street. Despite all that cooking, Ella retained her youthful, slim figure and paid careful attention to her appearance.

She was most beautiful in her white church suit. She positively glowed, the girls of the church observed. Mothers of the church were recognized on the third Sunday of every month, and the congregants identified Ella by her radiant white suit and hat. "Fashionable" and "in vogue" were descriptions often applied to her.

Nelse was a Sunday school superintendent and usher. A sharp dresser, most women he encountered described him as "tall, dark, and handsome"—even twenty years after his death.

Nelse wore his hair close cut and favored a fedora in public. Stacy Adams was his preferred shoe, and he took special pride in wearing starched white shirts—so stiff he could cut his neck on the collar. Or so they appeared.

The neighborhood watched him washing his car on Saturdays, the only day he'd take it out for a ride through the quarters of Hattiesburg. Whatever car was in his possession at the time was his pride and joy. After a loving morning of detailing, he'd hop into the vehicle, roll down the driver's side window, prop his arm on the door, and cruise slowly through the streets, over to Mobile Street, and down through the Bouie district—a handsome man in a fine ride. People noticed.

When Ella and Nelse bought their black-and-white television set, they placed it in their bedroom. No matter—the neighborhood children flocked to the Gaston's where they were allowed to sit on the floor and watch their favorite shows, such as *I Love Lucy, The Roy Rogers Show*, and *The Adventures of Ozzie and Harriet,* none of which featured a black protagonist.

Nelse bought a film that gave the illusion of color to cover the screen. Everything at the top was blue, in the middle everything was red, and on the bottom, green. However it looked, the Gastons had color TV—a neighborhood first.

Any television coverage of the civil rights struggles beginning to blossom around the country was often interrupted by "technical difficulties" conveniently applied by the local station owners.

There were plenty of street football games and a homemade version of baseball with a broomstick and tennis balls out in the "pasture" area of the neighborhood for the boys. Jacks, hopscotch, and bounce-the-board were the more sedate pastimes of neighborhood girls.

Rock throwing, sugar cane sucking, and riding to school in the old yellow school bus were all cherished memories of Lee Street for the Reverend P. C. Donald Sr. of Lexington, Kentucky, who wrote a memorial tribute in 1984 upon the death of Clifford Gaston, the middle son of Ella and Nelse.

Lee Street was a fine environment for nurturing children into self-confident adults willing to take a stand when the need arose.

The Reverend Donald recalled one incident in particular that provides insight into the Newman Quarters culture and, as he wrote, offers a glimpse of Clifford "in one of his finest moments":

> We were on our way home from school (Rowan High) on the city bus. Somehow, we had decided that it was our time to join the rest of the blacks around the country to make an overt physical protest by sitting on the front seats of the bus. And, just so happened, we [had] as a driver, just about the skinniest, ugliest, meanest, tobacco chewing white bus driver known to black folks in Hattiesburg. Everybody talked about how nasty he was to black people.
>
> But we were not disturbed at this bus driver's presence on this day; not one bit even though we knew he always carried a black jack in his pocket.

We were determined to sit up front and do our part for civil rights.

We did sit up front, and were told to get up and move back to the rear of the bus. But no one moved. Being a diehard redneck, the bus driver quickly slammed on his brakes and grabbed his black jack from his pocket.

Cliff, not being a Gandhi disciple as was Dr. Martin Luther King, jumped to his feet and raced toward the driver. He grabbed the driver in the collar and shoved him against the steering wheel, took his black jack from him and threw it out the window. Feeling somewhat naked and helpless, the bus driver took his seat and drove off. The incident was over in a few moments. We had won!

For the women of Newman Quarters, Saturdays were devoted to housekeeping, going to town to shop, going to the beauty shop, and getting themselves and their children ready for church the next day. For the men, Saturdays were mostly spent running the errands on the lists their wives gave them, peering intently under someone's open car hood, working on somebody else's honey-do list, or spending the afternoon at Nelse Gaston's backyard barber shop.

When the "incident" happened to the Gastons, the adults didn't talk about it in front of the little ones, but everyone knew something bad had happened to Mr. Nelse and Miz Ella. They all heard adults in church praying aloud over the Gastons' "trials and tribulations." The mothers whispered on the Dent's Grocery porch as if they thought someone was hiding under it listening to them. And the men were all afraid of the Ku Klux Klan, it seemed to the youngsters.

Until the decision was made to write it all down, even Nelse and Ella's own children had no idea of the extent of their parents' troubles.

The Cook

Nelse and Ella understood that the underpinning of a successful marriage is mutual respect. It is no wonder their marriage lasted sixty-two years, not only through everyday stresses and hardships of living as black people in a vehemently prejudicial state but also through one of the most harrowing crises any marriage could endure.

Once the children became somewhat self-sufficient, Ella and Nelse decided that the family would benefit if she worked outside their home. The Gastons wanted their children to go to college, and though Hattiesburg was a college town, there was little hope that the doors of the local institutions would be open to their children. Blacks were not allowed to enroll. Sending the children to a historically black university far away was almost impossible without a second income.

Ella's many skills included keeping little ones in line, but the gift in which she felt most confident was her cooking. She was certainly a renowned cook in her neighborhood, and she felt it would be only a little more trouble to cook for a hundred than it was for her eight—or for the numerous others who came trooping through her house during mealtimes or for those who came by her box in the churchyard. In 1955 Ella learned through a friend that there was an opening for a cook at the nearby Hattiesburg Convalescent Center on Bay Street. She applied and began work as a member of Mrs. Jewell McMahan's team.

Mrs. Mac, as they called her, was an exacting boss who expected her employees to keep their focus on the center's elderly residents. She was very serious about it. Nothing was too good for the patients; she personally saw to it that no detail was overlooked for those in her care. Mrs. Mac had a reputation for treating her employees with dignity and respect and as extended McMahan family members, but she meant business about caring for the residents of the Hattiesburg Convalescent Center.

Mrs. Mac expected everyone to work side by side, herself included, in caring for the residents. It didn't matter what color you were, she'd fire you immediately if you didn't take care of the most important people in the place. And the "most important people" didn't mean you or her.

It was pretty much unheard of in 1950s Mississippi for people of different races to work together as peers, not to mention use the same bathroom facilities. Mrs. Mac insisted that no distinction be drawn among her employees. They were all to carry on as equal partners in this important endeavor. They entered the same doors, ate at the same tables, and used the same toilets. Consequently, working at the center was a much sought-after occupation for a black person in Hattiesburg and an experience in equality for whites. Ella considered herself blessed.

The Hattiesburg white establishment shook its head.

Mrs. Mac carried on.

JEWELL'S STORY

The Lantern

Jewell Clark was making her first foray into Hattiesburg aboard a Southern Railway train very late on September 7, 1940. It was black as pitch.

A recent business education graduate of Bowling Green Business University, the twenty-one-year-old aspiring educator from the East Kentucky mountains of Hatfields and McCoys fame was on her way to Forrest County Agricultural High School in Brooklyn, Mississippi. It was her first teaching job.

She wore a sensible brown traveling suit, reasonable heels, and a smart, but not too flashy, hat. Her hair was dark and wavy, and she had smoothed it under just above her collar. Altogether, she looked like a schoolteacher, or so she hoped.

Jewell also wore a modest diamond ring that marked her as claimed. She had met her fiancé when they were both in their senior year at Bowling Green Business College. She viewed him as being higher than she in the social strata of Kentucky. She learned the ways of high society from him and how to go along with but not partake in some things, as she said. They became engaged, and he'd landed a job at Kalamazoo, Michigan, teaching business courses at a private school. She'd gone up to see him shortly after they had graduated, but there wasn't a job for her there. She needed one, they'd both decided, and she called their alma mater for help.

The lady at Bowling Green's placement office found the teaching job in Mississippi for her. "Now, it'll be different there," the counselor warned. Jewell was advised that she would likely have trouble with the food, and trouble with the lifestyle, but it was close to the "ocean," if she'd never been there. Plus, it paid so much better than teaching jobs up north. It seemed like a fun adventure, and Jewell Clark had never turned down an adventure.

It was midnight on Saturday when the shushing steam engine pulled in beside the longest stretch of passenger landing in the South. The Hattiesburg Depot on Newman Street was built in grand Italian Renaissance style with multipaned arched windows framed in fancy cast concrete, a red clay tile roof, and no expense spared in architectural appointments within. Its great hall stretched like a ballroom for a hundred feet with a soaring ceiling held aloft by acanthus-crowned columns over an inlaid floor.

The twenty-nine-year-old diamond of downtown Hattiesburg was a creation of the famed Frank P. Milburn, of Bowling Green, Kentucky, designer of capitols, courthouses, and public places across the Southeast. It had been commissioned by the Southern Railway Company.

Only three years earlier, some say rock-and-roll music was first recorded when "Blind" Roosevelt Graves, his brother Uaroy Graves, and pianist Cooney Vaughn, playing as the Mississippi Jook Band, recorded "Barbecue Bust" and "Dangerous Women" for the American Record Company right there at the station. The riffs and runs over a thumping beat marked the music as real rock and roll, *Rolling Stone* magazine declared decades later.

On this night, though, the station was dead silent.

At over fourteen thousand square feet on one level, the depot seemed to embody all the possibility of a city that billed itself as "the Hub." Rail, river, and roads converged to make Hattiesburg the gateway to New Orleans, Mobile, Meridian, Natchez, Jackson, and Gulfport. This fact was announced from a big, round, lighted sign atop the Ross Building downtown. The sign was strategically positioned so that night train passengers would have no doubt they were entering a special place from whence they could go anywhere they wanted–anywhere that is, except Jewell's destination, Brooklyn, Mississippi, in the middle of this night.

Hattiesburg was situated in south central Mississippi, and its chief economic engine was the pine tree. Great stands of virgin long-leaf yellow pine had been harvested since the 1890s in clear-cutting exercises requiring strong men, stout oxen, and heavy rails to move millions of board feet of lumber annually. When the depot was built, Mississippi was ranked third in the nation for lumber production, behind Washington and Louisiana. Commercial logging was big business, and the depot demonstrated just how important the lumber business was to Hattiesburg.

Jewell had been warned before they arrived that she'd missed her connection and that the train to Brooklyn wouldn't come 'til morning. She could spot no one at the station. Jewell considered her options and decided just to spend the night in the dimly lit waiting room. There was no arguing with a train schedule.

She prepared to wait on one of the straight-backed benches. The seats were hard golden oak and about wide enough for two small people or one large one. She sat her suitcase beside her, stared straight ahead, and waited.

Sitting in the dark, steamy silence of the depot's cramped waiting area, Jewell Clark was far from the cool, clear air of Kentucky, though the tough determination she inherited from the mountain folk was with her this night. She was the granddaughter of soldiers—one a Rebel, the other a Yankee—and she was taught from an early age to fear nothing. A hard backbone, a keen eye, and a willingness to say what you mean and back it up were desired qualities in Appalachia. In Inez, Kentucky, just off Tug Fork, being self-assured and unafraid was as natural as breathing. And, just because Jewell was a woman was no excuse to behave any differently. She certainly wasn't going to panic. She had her pistol in her purse.

The yellow glow of an oil lantern began to interrupt the dark. The door swung open, and there stood a tall, black man in an official-looking train station uniform. He held his lantern up to see her face.

They looked at each other. It would be another forty years before a black man in Hattiesburg, Mississippi, would feel comfortable being alone with a white woman in circumstances like these. People had been lynched for less. In fact, the records showed that more than 450 black Americans had been lynched in Mississippi from 1882 to 1930, events still fresh enough to make a solid difference in how black men related to white women. And those were the lynchings that had been recorded—there was no telling how many had actually occurred. Indeed, matters of racial separation were taken very seriously in the woodsy county named Forrest, in honor of the reputed leader of the Ku Klux Klan.

There is a worn-out but true saying in politics: "Perception is reality." Such was the case for Nathan Bedford Forrest in the waning years of his life and most certainly by 1940.

Forrest was a man whose name conjured up either fear or reverence in Mississippi, depending on one's heritage. For those who glorified "The Lost Cause," Forrest was a sainted icon. He was a masterful guerrilla war strategist whose battle prowess was feared by his enemies and emulated afterward by generations of soldiers here and abroad. For those whose parents or grandparents were enslaved, however, he was viewed as a brutal and conscienceless murderer who issued orders to shoot down black prisoners of war at Fort Pillow.

The Klan's ingenious use of white sheets to disguise themselves as the spirits of departed Confederate soldiers was widely credited as Forrest's brainchild. Grown men prowled through the night wearing ghost costumes and calling each other names like Cyclops and Grand Wizard. Perhaps they thought they were preying upon the unsophisticated black citizenry's extreme superstition, but, in fact, the fear displayed by their victims was genuine. The pain and horror inflicted by the "ghosts" were completely real; beatings, lynchings, draggings, and fires were the thugs' preferred *modus operandi*.

Two weeks before Jewell arrived there, United States Senator Theodore Bilbo, who was running for reelection, came to Hattiesburg to deliver a stump speech. His campaign placed a prominent advertisement in the *Hattiesburg American* exhorting local citizens to come "hear Senator Bilbo under shade trees at Hattiesburg at one o'clock Monday afternoon, August 26." Number 17 in the senator's advertised list of twenty-nine favorite public service accomplishments was "Helped to kill un-American anti-lynching bill." He was a very proud white Mississippian.

At the Hattiesburg train depot in the middle of the night where a black man stood alone with a strange white woman, these issues lurked like unseen "haints" in the corners of the darkened depot.

For the late night passenger, he was one of only a few black men she'd been this close to in her lifetime. There were no black people in Inez, Kentucky, that she had ever realized, at least. If there were any in Bowling Green, the former center of Kentucky's Confederate government, she hadn't been aware. There was this friend of her father's who'd come up from the state capital at Frankfort to discuss government business. He and her father met at the family dining room table occasionally, she could remember.

She had experienced some bad behaviors related to skin color, though. At college, she and her girlfriends attended a couple of ballgames with some male students who were of Asian Indian descent and so darker than the ladies. Jewell's group was taunted and jeered by a bunch of drunken white boys.

They said, "Hey, did you bring your nigger with you this time?"

Jewell gave them the shoulder and turned up her nose. "Yes, I sure did. Isn't he cute?"

Her companion said he didn't want her to have to take the abuse. They didn't bother her at all, she said, and she didn't change what she did one bit.

"Let me do it," she said. "They'll be yelling at you next if I don't."

And that was the sum total of her personal experience with overt racial prejudice before she came to Mississippi.

Something told the railroad man that she wasn't local. She was way too composed for that.

"Ma'am, you're not from Mississippi, are you?" he asked.

She told him she was from Kentucky and had missed her connection down to Brooklyn. When he cautioned her that it may be dangerous for her to be in the depot alone, she admitted she didn't know what else to do.

"Well, I can take you up to the Southern Hotel," he offered, describing the place as old but open all night with a nice restaurant. Like most rail companies of the time, the Southern line offered hotels along the route for its overnight passengers who were making connections at odd hours.

Okay, she said, but she didn't ask him how they'd get there.

Picking up her suitcase and holding the lantern in the other hand, he guided her out of the waiting room, off the platform, and onto the rails. With the lantern swinging back and forth to light the way, the two of them pressed into the night, stepping along the creosoted railroad ties toward the Southern Hotel. There they went—a white girl and a black man walking down the railroad tracks in the middle of the night in Hattiesburg, Mississippi, in 1940, and she didn't even know where she was going.

Southern Hospitality

When Jewell and her unlikely escort arrived at the Southern Hotel, it appeared that the inn, although old and a little rundown, was well furnished—in the lobby at least.

Jewell looked around appreciatively at the upholstered chairs in the lobby and the large adjacent dining room. Thumbed-through magazines would keep her awake. The gentleman with the lantern explained her situation to the desk people, who assured him they would keep an eye on her in the safety of the lobby.

What Jewell didn't know, but the locals likely did, was that a three-state all points bulletin had been issued for thirty-six escaped convicts who had bolted from the Cummins Penitentiary at Grady, Arkansas, on Labor Day. So far, some of the escapees had kidnapped and held hostage one set of high schoolers and a group of college kids over in Louisiana. A number of those on the lam had been shot, and others had been captured and taken back to Arkansas. The *Hattiesburg American* had been full of lurid details on the kidnappings and captures and even included a picture of one escapee suffering from his wounds while law enforcement officers posed proudly for the camera with their weapons. Jewell had arrived during the height of a local panic that wild-eyed, escaped convicts might burst through the door demanding hostages at any second.

The desk clerk peered anxiously Jewell's way, but she was determined to stay upright there in the lobby until time to leave for Brooklyn. She sat for about an hour, glancing through the magazines and trying to stay awake. She was glad that she had only her little suitcase and essentials with her instead of having to drag big trunks around. She had shipped the bulk of her possessions separately and knew they would be arriving a day or two behind her.

She wasn't in the least concerned for her things, though. Jewell had learned the fine art of traveling succinctly from a friend she'd made in Bowling Green. He wrote restaurant critiques and travel books and represented Smithfield Hams—juxtaposed vocations that seemed perfectly reasonable at the time. His name was Duncan Hines, and the college would invite him in occasionally to teach students how to travel. Mr. Hines and his wife had often hosted Jewell and her friends for dinners and discussions. Stumbling around over the big hams to get to the Hines dining room was something she never forgot. She also never forgot that you could travel, see the world, and eat well on limited funds, if you knew the shortcuts. Mr. Hines was full of shortcuts.

In the lobby, Jewell became suddenly aware of a handsome businessman in his mid-forties watching her as he came down the stairs. Approaching her, he patted her knee. *Uh-oh,* she said to herself.

The man graciously offered her the use of his room because he was leaving, and he held out its key. She politely declined. Later, as she sat stoically in the lobby, the prospect of lying down, even if only for an hour or so, became more and more appealing.

Jewell approached the desk clerk to remind her about the gentleman's offer of his room. The lady at the desk said absolutely not; Jewell couldn't stay in a dirty room. They'd find her a clean one, which they did—kind of.

The room was a shock to Jewell, who had been reared by a very particular mother when it came to cleanliness. To her eyes, the place was very poorly fixed. This was due, she suspected, to the fact that the Southern Lines weren't the "big lines." She figured the accommodations granted to delayed rail travelers were directly proportional to the wealth of the line providing them. After retrieving clean bath linens and a sheet to spread out over the bed so she could at least lie down without touching anything, Jewell slept a fitful few hours. She woke up early, anxious to meet the train.

Taking a donut and coffee compliments of the house, as recommended by Mr. Hines, Jewell asked if she'd have to take out over the tracks again to catch the train, but Southern gallantry was not to be denied. "No," they said at the desk. "We'll take you," and so they did, by car.

The hotel had bestowed its personal brand of that famous Mississippi hospitality on the unruffled little traveler from Kentucky.

Preparing for War

Jewell arrived at the station just in time to see her gallant businessman from the night before board the train. He nodded almost imperceptibly. She nodded back.

Things looked different there in the daylight. Under the vast awning, people were scurrying about, tending to the business of travel. Some were in uniform; others were in their Sunday best. Most everybody was white except the porters. Any dark-skinned passengers were boarding way down the line of cars, adhering to the Jim Crow laws that demanded the races travel separately. She didn't see her kindly escort from the night before.

Settling herself into a hard-padded seat, Jewell asked the conductor about Brooklyn. It wasn't far, he said, only about twenty miles.

Three years before, the Works Project Administration (WPA) researchers proclaimed Brooklyn to be one of the largest communities in Forrest County besides Hattiesburg. It was home to a residential secondary school–Forrest County Agricultural High School–where Jewell was joining the faculty.

How the little hamlet came to bear the name of a storied borough of New York City was a tale rooted in antebellum segregation between white landowners and their slaves. As chronicled by the WPA writers,

> A man by the name of Griffin settled in what was then Perry County and brought with him a large number of slaves. The slaves lived in an excluded division of the plantation, and the owner and others would speak of the colored quarters as New York, because of the extra size of it. As long as any colored people lived in that vicinity, it was called New York. When the Gulf and Ship Island Railroad was established and a sufficient number of people moved to the site now known as Brooklyn to justify naming it, someone suggested Brooklyn because of its proximity to New York. When the Government granted permission to establish a post office at the place, it was called Brooklyn for the above mentioned reason.

It was a noisy departure. People were yelling above the din of the dainty steam engine grinding her gears to begin the journey south all the way to Gulfport. The Gulf and Ship Island engineer pulled the whistle cord for two long moans, signaling that the train was about to proceed. He made sure to pull the cord just so. That way, everyone within earshot would know he was the man behind the machine.

On the way out of Hattiesburg, the train carried Jewell through the city's oldest residential area, where elegant mansions of Piney Woods lumber barons saluted one another across Short Bay Street and the staid, white Bay Street Presbyterian church sat solemnly facing the tracks. Included in the panorama slipping along beside her window were houses sitting on property she would one day own under the Hattiesburg Convalescent Center. Indeed, places she passed on her first morning out of Hattiesburg would be the same scenery she would later pass on her commute to and from work, day after day, for fifty-four years. Right now, though, Brooklyn was the only thing in her sights.

Not far beyond the tranquil, residential quiet of Sunday morning neighborhoods, the train thrust its way into the dusty chaos of a military base undergoing an enormous growth surge.

There were loud machines, men rushing about, and buildings under construction. It was Camp Shelby, and "they" were bringing in the troops, a fellow passenger told Jewell.

The day before her arrival, Mississippi governor Paul B. Johnson Sr. had signed papers turning over the state's 5,185 acres within the training ground to the federal government as a permanent installation. The frenzied construction site was under intense pressure to be ready for the soldiers when war came. By the fall of 1940, everyone knew that it was just a matter of time. The *Hattiesburg American* had been devoting its front page news to the European war theater for most of the past year. The countdown was on. Camp Shelby, established in 1917 as a training camp for World War I troops, would be ready for the next big blow.

Hattiesburg bootleggers' reputation for distilling the worst moonshine available to the soldiers had been the subject of an August newspaper article in the *Hattiesburg American* entitled "Mississippi Booze the Worst, Say Soldiers-With-a-Thirst." A number of soldiers had been seriously sickened from the stuff, the reports said. Mississippi was, after all, a "dry"state, and those who chose to indulge in the pleasures of alcohol did so at their own peril.

The dust and clamor of pressing construction fell away as the train sped past open pastures and remnants of great pine forests, laid bare by the intense fifty-year harvest that had developed the area now known as the Pine Belt. The remaining woods and fields were mostly curled and faded around the edges from the unrelenting steam bath of the dying summer, but along the ditches were boisterous parties of purple sedge, blue mistflower, bright yellow black-eyed Susans, and crimson smilax, guarded every now and then by a stand of tall waving goldenrods. Once in a while, you could get a glimpse of a delicate cardinal flower in a ditch overshadowed by sweeping stalks of wild elderberry with their hanging black fruit. Orange trumpet creeper punctuated sunny high spots, and wild lavender aster sprinkled the yellowing grass like lacy snow. This new countryside didn't look like the mountainscape of Kentucky, but it was pretty just the same.

This was a time of deep poverty in Mississippi. Although some of the country had begun to pull itself out of the ravenous gully of the Great Depression, times were still hard here. Only seven years earlier, on a single day in April, forty thousand farms were on the auction block to be sold for back taxes. The already stretched state government suddenly found itself to be the caretaker of millions of acres of its citizens' land. Because the population was predominantly rural and therefore agricultural, at least country folk had food. They may have had newspaper in their windows, stuffed cardboard in their shoes, and wore flour-sack dresses, but they largely possessed an ability to raise and preserve crops, tend producing animals, and generally persevere.

For the extremely impoverished, the stark social dividing lines between black and white were blurred, according to Mississippi civil rights leader Aaron Henry. In his autobiography, Henry noted the congenial relationships that wretched poverty sometimes bestowed upon Mississippians of different races: "We had a common bond in our impoverishment, and color made no difference between us—no segregation and no white supremacy. We all stood in the same line to get our goods at the commissary."

Nevertheless, although mired in the depths of poverty, a group of fierce and proud white people yearned for the days of old, when they imagined their forefathers living in huge white mansions, served by humble black slaves. While most antebellum white Mississippians were in fact dirt farmers, laborers, or merchants with few or no slaves, many grandchildren of the vanquished Confederacy fancied themselves to be a part of a lost aristocracy and so demanded to be respected as such by their black neighbors, even in 1940. It was, for this group, preferable to be above somebody than beneath everybody, and children and grandchildren of slaves seemed to form the perfect class of underlings.

Hardly anything demonstrates whites' postwar need for dominance more than the voting franchise section of the 1890 state constitution that was crafted around the idea of racial dominance and submission via the polling place. By 1896, the state's Supreme Court let the cat out of the bag, so to speak, when it admitted as much:

> The Mississippi constitutional convention of 1890,
> wrote the court, swept the circle of expedients

to obstruct the exercise of the franchise by the Negro race. By reason of its previous condition of servitude and dependence, this race had acquired or accentuated certain particularities of habit, of temperament and of character, which clearly distinguished it, as a race, from that of the whites—a patient, docile people, but careless, landless, and migratory within narrow limits, without forethought, and *its criminal members given rather to furtive offenses than to the robust crimes of the whites. Restrained by the federal constitution from discriminating against the negro race, the convention discriminated against its characteristics and the offenses to which its weaker members were prone. ...* Burglary, theft, arson, and obtaining money under false pretenses were declared to be disqualifications [for voting], while robbery and murder, and other crimes in which violence was the principal ingredient, were not.

The Constitution of 1890 was still the solid law of the land in Mississippi in 1940.

It was an easy thing to enforce a strict class code when the underlying structure of state government and its statutes protected the societal divide so securely. The foot of the state was firmly planted on the necks of its inhabitants who were least equipped to resist.

Not all white people in Mississippi subjected people of color to degradation and dangerous behaviors for sure. However, for the most part, those who didn't formed a silent wall around those who did.

Brooklyn

Placidly riding on the slow steam train down to Brooklyn, Jewell had no way of knowing that hers would be a white voice raised in defiant opposition to practices of the "Southern Way of Life" in mid-twentieth century Mississippi—or that her fight alongside her friend would be noted in the state's courtrooms for all time.

In Inez, Kentucky, there was no need for racial divides that she could discern, and matters of racial discrimination were certainly nothing to be discussed in her household. Her grandparents' generation had already drawn guns over the topic, and her mother's father had won. What was actually discussed at the Clark family dinner table was the mandate to treat all people with dignity and respect.

The slowing train approached a huddle of buildings while the conductor bellowed, "Brooklyn! Brooklyn!" Then with two long whistles, the train sped back up with no stop, no boarding passengers, and, significantly, no disembarking passengers.

Stunned, Jewell looked around in confusion. She was supposed to wear glasses, but she kept them tucked into a book and only wore them when she needed to see the blackboard. Whether she actually saw it or not, Jewell realized that the long-awaited Brooklyn had just flown past her window. She pulled on a cord made just for passenger emergencies. This was definitely an emergency. She pulled the string hard, ringing the bells, and the train came to a grudging halt.

"I've gotta get off at Brooklyn!" she proclaimed to the conductor, whose neck was beginning to bulge over the collar of his uniform.

"We've already gone through Brooklyn," he observed.

"Take me back," she said.

He looked around for rescue. There was no one else to turn to, just one squarely determined young woman with hands on her hips and blue-green eyes staring straight into his. She wasn't budging.

"Hold on. We're gonna back up," the resigned conductor finally announced. And so they did.

With three short whistle bursts, the engineer began to snake the train backward along the rails toward Brooklyn.

Backing up a train wasn't completely unheard of. In fact, it presented a great opportunity to showcase an engineer's expertise as a professional. This day, the delicate dance was being performed on the tiny Brooklyn stage before a miniscule audience.

What seemed like five miles later, they all came to a stop in front of the little welcoming center—a white wooden building, about ten feet square and rather tall with both front and back doors wide open and some benches inside. As usual, no one was there to greet Jewell Clark.

She waited for the train to leave the Brooklyn station the second time that morning, and, with little brown suitcase in hand, Jewell gingerly stepped across the tracks to the Brooklyn Mercantile Store. A squat red brick building, the store's tin porch roof sheltered benches outside, providing a neighborly gathering spot. Surprisingly for a Sunday morning in the Bible Belt, the place showed some life.

Inside the store, Jewell introduced herself as the new teacher needing a ride to school—right now.

Ushered down the street to the pharmacy with the assurance that someone there would give her a ride, by then she was so hoarse that she could barely speak. Jewell was surprised when Mr. Walker, the pharmacist, immediately began concocting a potion for her throat as soon as she started describing her urgent need for a lift. If there was a place to pick for a young woman traveling alone with strangers, it appeared that Mississippi was definitely the place.

Stepping out onto the store's stoop, Jewell saw a tiny parade of dark-haired, olive-skinned young women headed her way.

"You teacher? You teacher? You *our* teacher!"

Their chaperone offered an explanation. "These are the girls you'll be supervising in the dormitory. They are down here going to church today, and they wanted to meet the new teacher. Oh, and they're mostly from Honduras. "

Word traveled faster here than in Inez, Jewell thought.

She attempted to tell them that she'd see them later, summoning the few Spanish words she knew. They repaid her with a little song.

Not only was the school in Brooklyn a boarding high school for Mississippians, but well-to-do Latin Americans sent their sons and daughters there to study in a protected environment and absorb American culture in a controlled setting.

Years later, the University of Southern Mississippi in Hattiesburg boasted a thriving population of Central American students–children of privilege–whose parents may have based their offspring's higher education choices on the reputation of the Piney Woods formed a generation earlier, in part, at Brooklyn.

With her business degree, Jewell was hired to teach female students at the agricultural school how to type, take shorthand, write letters, and generally survive in the male-dominated world of a modern office. She'd wind up teaching them a few other things too–like how to leave a lasting impression on your boss the first time he sees you.

"Hal?" Mr. Walker stuck his head out of the door in the direction of a pickup truck slouching out front. "How about giving this young lady a ride up to the school? She's the new school ma'am." Jewell knew the superintendent was supposed to have been there to meet her, but, as appeared standard during this trip, nothing was going as planned.

Hal worked for the pharmacist, Jewell figured out. He and a friend were hanging around the store in a ratty old truck. They said they'd take her–more Mississippi hospitality. Taking a deep breath, she climbed in with her suitcase, moving Hal's delighted passenger over to the middle. It was very tight in that truck.

No sooner had she rolled up the window–hair trumped temperature–than she heard *knock, knock, knock*. A man stood there with a frown on his face and a suit on his body, and he peered through the window at her. She rolled it down.

"Are you Miss Clark?" he asked.

"Yes, sir."

"What are you doing in this truck?"

"The superintendent didn't meet me. These men are giving me a ride to the school."

"I am the superintendent. You can't ride around with these drunks. This is a bad way to start out."

They looked at each other.

"Well, sir, it's your fault. You didn't come get me. I had no other way to get to the school."

He stepped back. Teachers usually didn't talk to him that way. His name was Alan Mauldin. Good looking with an athlete's physique and a full head of hair, he appeared to be about forty years old. To Jewell, he sported a real teachery attitude–*real* teachery.

Mr. Mauldin likely had more on his mind than transporting a feisty first-year teacher. School started the next day, and he, like every other public school administrator in the state, was dealing with the public outcry over Governor Paul B. Johnson's signing of the free textbook law. It was all over the newspapers, and legislators who had opposed the move were taking every opportunity to thrash equally those who had passed it and those who were charged with implementing the new system. There was more than one red-faced meeting held to bat the issue back and forth as school openings were bearing down onto the dog days of summer. It was an affront to the free enterprise system and smacked of socialism, the detractors said. To make it even worse, the books were late, which meant that meaningful class activity would be delayed and the rest of the semester would be spent trying to catch up. A lawsuit contesting the constitutionality of the act had already been filed and rejected, and now Attorney Forrest B. Jackson of Hattiesburg, representing "three Mississippians," had sought an injunction to prohibit implementation of the statute. Final arguments were scheduled for Monday. The White System Inc. of Hattiesburg was advertising that free schoolbooks would not eliminate all of the expenses of getting children off to school and offered parents education loans that could be paid in monthly installments to ease the expense.

It was a silent five-minute ride to the school, traveling north on the Brooklyn-to-McLaurin road running along the G&SI railroad tracks. Jewell had seen this scenery before—just that morning, as a matter of fact.

The car turned onto a drive laid out to make the most of a long, scenic approach to the majestic art deco educational center standing proudly on the crest of a hill. The building was a symmetrical two-story structure showcasing fancy brickwork juxtaposed against straightforward, decorative embellishments typical of the style. A center fretwork of cast concrete, stylized cornstalks served as an imposing headpiece for the main entrance. Above the cornstalks was the embossed image of a farmer working in the field; below was a depiction of the machinery used to process the corn. Distinctive lamps bearing crown ornaments reminiscent of the Statue of Liberty's framed the walkway as a welcoming gesture onto campus.

Cast frescoes fronting the building's east and west wings portrayed what was apparently believed to be gender-appropriate renditions of the school's fields of study. "Home Science" featured a goddess-like woman in a sun-bathed yard with a quaint house in the background, hens and biddies at her feet, and a spinning wheel nearby. "Agriculture" showed a majestic man gazing proudly at his farm with a cornucopia of produce at his feet and the machinery necessary for processing it close by. These images foretold the school's social order as strictly enforced by its superintendent–girls on one end, boys on the other.

Established in 1911, FCAHS was a world unto itself. Everybody–faculty and students–lived on campus. Keeping that world under control was a challenge, especially when a goodly portion of the student body came from other cultures. The Latin American parents who sent their daughters to the school deep in the Piney Woods of Mississippi expected the same strict oversight of their children's courting lives as they would have imposed at home.

Cows and sheep grazed placidly on well-groomed pastures surrounding the campus. A paddling of ducks floated lazily across a dark lake surrounded by tall pines.

The whole place was pretty impressive for a girl from Appalachia. As they maneuvered along a gravel drive to the women's dormitory in back, Mr. Mauldin issued instructions. She should introduce herself to the house matron, get a room, and meet him in his office at 2:30 that afternoon.

At 2:31, he started in on her.

"Our teachers don't behave like you did, getting in a car with a drunk ..." he lectured.

She didn't want to hear any more about it, she said. After all, if he'd been on time, she wouldn't have been in the truck in the first place.

Stymied, Mr. Mauldin went into numerous detailed rules about keeping female students out of sight and therefore out of mind of their male counterparts. She could *not* take the girls in front of the boys' dormitory. They could *not* go to the lake by walking beside the boys' dormitory. Instead, they were to troop out onto the highway to get to the lake, a requirement Jewell thought singularly ridiculous.

Girls could *not* have dates on the campus. *But* if they were with anybody on Sunday afternoons in the lobby, they must be supervised *all* of the time–same for outside in the yard.

She went to breakfast on Monday morning and sat with her students. The first question of the day was, "Did you really get in a truck with a drunk?"

"Oh, yes," she answered with a wink. "Just don't tell the superintendent!"

Jewell and her charges had gathered up to a long table where food was served family style from bowls placed in the middle of the table. It was all dispensed in big hunks–butter, ham, and scrambled eggs. One of the bowls held something entirely unfamiliar, a mound of white stuff. Everybody else was digging in and putting butter and salt on the clumps they'd portioned out, Jewell observed. She suspected it was rice, but it was, she discovered, a bowl of grits.

"What's a grit?" she asked. Nobody could tell her. She tried it, found it to be tasteless, and eventually settled for a gigantic biscuit and some fatback bacon. The lady at Bowling Green had been right. The food was problematic.

Lunch was even more alarming. Just about everything on the table was new to her–collard and turnip roots, greens, okra, and cowpeas. She'd seen the black-eyed peas before, but they were only for the livestock where she was from. The "okree" was a slimy mess. She'd never heard of turnips or collards. She finally ate some turnip root and drank some tea, all the while longing for broccoli and cabbage. She'd surely keep her figure in this place.

Jewell came to appreciate one person in particular in the food service area. His name was Mr. Mahew, the very large black cook, whose skill as a dessert chef overshadowed all the strange vegetables and country-style eating manners of the dining hall. He turned out great cakes, pies, puddings, cobblers, and sweet rolls. Mr. Mahew was well known and loved by all, even if he failed to show up occasionally for Sunday dinner after an extra-vivacious Saturday night.

On Tuesday, another new teacher arrived–Mr. Mauldin was in double trouble. Pauline Crouch was also from a Kentucky hamlet, about sixty miles from Inez. Pauline and Jewell traded home stories, compared acquaintances and family members, and concluded that it was a miracle they hadn't known each other before, considering they had so much in common. Suddenly Jewell didn't feel so alone. The two young women from the mountains became inseparable.

Things didn't lighten up much between Miss Clark and Superintendent Mauldin. She got in trouble for letting her charges shoot baskets in the gym at night. She got in trouble for taking the girls to the lakeside and letting them take the shortcut back to their rooms–past the boys dorm. She got in trouble for leaving the lobby for a minute or two when two couples were inside. She was criticized for the number of supplies required for her commerce classes, such as typewriter ribbons, paper, and the like–things necessary to her subject matter, she insisted.

Mountain Ethics

Jewell wasn't one to submit to rules she deemed unnecessary or silly. That attitude didn't start at Forrest County Agricultural High School, and it wouldn't end there either.

The Clarks were a prominent family in the tiny mountain village of Inez, named for the daughter of a nearby postmaster in 1873. The town was the county seat of Martin County and bordered West Virginia. When Jewell left for the Deep South, a new limestone courthouse was nearly complete. The building, which would eventually serve as the iconic image of the mining town, was built of rocks quarried from the nearby mountains. Local lumber composed the interior structure and embellishments. In 1940, the townspeople were eagerly anticipating completion of this striking monument to their town's importance.

"You've gotta lead from the front" was a Clark family axiom.

Both of Jewell's parents held college degrees. Lutie Delong Clark, daughter of a state representative, was a professional educator. Blaine Clark also started out as a teacher but served many years as an attorney for the commonwealth, several as county attorney, a term as a state senator, one as a judge, and four years on the Board of Regents of Morehead State Teachers College. He was also an ordained Methodist minister.

Occasionally, Jewell and her pals would go across the river to dance, burrowed under the hay on the back of a friend's old pickup named the Tomcat. The "river" was the Big Sandy separating Kentucky from West Virginia. A tributary of the Big Sandy, Tug Fork, was what literally separated the McCoys from the Hatfields.

Although the famous feud was allegedly over for a couple of decades by the time Jewell was in high school, the spirit of the quick-tempered, stubborn, and fearless mountaineer persona was still the most important cultural motif for the region. Carrying a gun was as normal as wearing clothes.

Before Jewell was born, old Devil Anse Hatfield himself ventured over the Tug Fork into McCoy territory to pay a visit to Blaine Clark's home one night with a legal problem. Devil Anse was one of many characters who came and went from her parents' door seeking help from her father, depending on whether he was a preacher, teacher, defense lawyer, district attorney, or state senator at the time.

Government agents occasionally showed up in Inez looking for moonshine. Whenever the "foreigners" were in town, Blaine knew he'd have a glut of cases if he didn't sound the alarm to a number of his clients, so he would disappear into the night to let his clients know to expect visitors.

Lutie took every opportunity to teach her daughters the fine points of living distinctly. First of all, one's home should be orderly and prepared to receive visitors at all times. No flashy clothes or loud perfume for the Clark women. Always display the best manners at the table and elsewhere, and carry yourself like you're somebody important because you are, no matter your station in life. Do not be common or cheap, and, above all, treat well those who help you. You're not a bit better than that person who is serving your dinner.

In a world where appearing to be self-confident is half the battle of success, Jewell learned that women were required to present an even more impressive image than their male counterparts if they were going to prosper in a male-dominated society.

Bryce

During the first semester at FCAHS, Jewell befriended industrial arts teacher Orville Thomas. His dad was head of the industrial arts program at Mississippi Southern College in Hattiesburg. Since Jewell and Orville were both attached to others, dating wasn't part of their equation.

The teachers went with the other faculty singles as a group to roller skate in Purvis, eat ice cream at Mr. Walker's pharmacy in downtown Brooklyn, take in a picture show, visit the hamburger joint, or go out dancing, Jewell's favorite thing to do. The friends felt the spirit of Mr. Mauldin on them wherever they went, and so their activities were tame.

Dancing was all the rage, and couples were competing for prizes all over the country. South Mississippi was no exception. The *Hattiesburg American* reported that a couple from Lumberton had gained national attention by dancing the shag all the way up Highway 11 to Hattiesburg. The man said he was fine; the woman reported a few blisters.

La congo was another popular dance, and Jewell made sure she knew all the moves. She'd honed her dance-floor skills in both high school and college, dancing with the Bowling Green president every time she could. Despite being located in a Southern Baptist-infused culture that frowned heavily upon the art, the young teachers from FCAHS spent abundant time on the dance floors of the Piney Woods.

Except for a couple of memorable excursions out with another female teacher who had too much to drink, Jewell found the young single life at Forrest County Agricultural High School to be unremarkable—so far.

After spending a cold Thanksgiving weekend alone at the school with fire and food provisions left for them by the kindly cook, Mr. Mahew, Jewell and Pauline took a slow, steam train ride home to the mountains for the Christmas holidays. When the Kentucky ladies returned to work, they found that the school in the woods had undergone a significant change. Orville informed them that a couple of new teachers had joined the staff, one of them being Bryce McMahan.

Fresh from finishing his degree at Mississippi Southern College, Bryce was killing some time before he went into active military duty, like so many of his peers. He was broad-chested and tan, and he carried himself with the confidence of a veteran football player.

His hazel eyes were friendly, and when he smiled, his dimples ran the length of his cheeks. Jewell took one look at him and knew her engagement was likely over.

She confided to Pauline, "I want that one from Hattiesburg." That was okay; Pauline was eyeing the other one.

From back up in Hattiesburg, FCAHS seemed the perfect destination for rowdy high school-age boys. Like their Latin American counterparts, the local parents, wanting to provide their offspring with a structured, disciplined, and shielded educational environment, were all too glad to give their sons the opportunity to go to boarding school. No matter that the school wasn't "up East" or even Chamberlain-Hunt over at Port Gibson, the consensus was that the agricultural school was a tremendous training ground for young men to be leaders in their communities. Plus, it offered the added advantage of corralling the mavericks away from the mischief of the Hub City.

Bryce was a former student from up the road in Eatonville. After a stint in the boxing ring and on the gridiron at Perkinston Junior College, he had come home to Hattiesburg to graduate with a bachelor's degree and wound up back at Brooklyn.

The young teachers met for a Coke before class most days. One morning, Bryce queried, "What y'all gonna do this weekend?"

"I wish I knew," Jewell countered.

The men decided to flip a quarter to determine their dates. Bryce got Jewell.

For the remainder of the semester, Bryce and Jewell became as inseparable as they could manage under the stern, watchful eyes of Mr. Mauldin.

The next logical progression for the couple was a visit to meet the McMahan family.

Like the Clarks, the McMahan family had a strong history of leadership. Hoyt McMahan married Effie May Johnson, daughter of an Alabama state senator, and moved from Cleburne County, Alabama, to the Eatonville area of Forrest County in the early 1920s to carve out a place for his family. By 1940, the McMahans owned one of the largest dairies in the area. Anyone who knows a thing about the dairy business knows it is an unrelenting, demanding, and physically exhausting way to provide for a family. The McMahan children thrived in the challenging environment. Bryce was the oldest, followed by sister Willadene, brother J. K., and the twins—brother Burnell and sister Lavelle, born on St. Patrick's Day, 1924.

Jewell found herself in the midst of a clan of Scots who rivaled anything she'd ever seen in Kentucky's wild mountains. They were boisterous, adventurous, and fearless. The McMahans just never seemed to back away from challenges. She liked that.

Bryce's challenge was to land the prize away from his unseen rival up north. He was up to it.

Eventually, Jewell and Bryce were spending more time alone together. Whereas previously the teacher troupe traveled together in one car, Bryce managed to secure a private ride just for the two of them.

They were getting real serious. One Sunday night on the way back from visiting with the McMahan clan, Bryce pulled off the road at Cypress Hill.

She asked him what he was doing.

"I thought this would be a good night to park here," he offered. She agreed.

"What are you going to tell me?" she wanted to know.

"I want to ask you if you'll marry me."

"But I'm already engaged," she stated the obvious.

They contemplated their situation for a while.

"Well, since you don't have a ring, do you want to use this one?" she finally asked, slipping the little diamond ring from her finger.

"Yes."

And the man with the massive hands delicately slipped the ring back onto her third finger, left hand. It was sealed.

The couple kept their news to themselves, just trying to last the school year without a dramatic ending. It seemed like a good plan at the time.

Late in the spring, Jewell and Bryce were once again returning from a visit to Eatonville when Bryce pulled Jewell over for a quick good-night kiss. The next thing they knew, the car was off the road and rolling down an embankment on the approach to the school.

Bryce crawled out and lifted Jewell out behind him. Then he issued a set of instructions. She was to go through the field and into the side door of the women's building, find the matron, tell her what happened, and get in the bed. She needed to deny everything to anybody else.

Jewell implemented the plan.

In about thirty minutes, Elizabeth Fletcher was banging on Jewell's door. Her fellow teacher was the anxious bearer of terrible news. Bryce had been in a wreck.

Jewell played the part—dutifully throwing on her clothes, crying, graciously accepting all condolences, and running down to the accident scene, where she discovered the car miraculously turned upright. Bryce stood sheepishly beside it.

The next day, Mr. Mauldin summoned Bryce with information stating that he and Jewell had been seen leaving campus together the previous afternoon. Bryce made up some story about going to get cigarettes, but Mr. Mauldin was never convinced. He stated his suspicions over and over for the remainder of the semester.

On the last day of school, Bryce and Jewell made an appointment to meet with Mr. Maulding in his office. They told him the truth about the accident, and Mr. Mauldin learned that he was not crazy, after all.

Attention, America!

After the end of the school year, Bryce received orders to report to Fort Dix, and Jewell reported to Fort Knox. She had asked for a fun summer job, and her father had helped secure this one. Whatever, she knew she wasn't going back to Brooklyn.

In August, Jewell called Inez High School, asked them if they had an opening, and became the business teacher at her alma mater. She was living at home with her parents while waiting on her wedding day, which was yet to be determined. One Sunday morning after Thanksgiving, she was dallying in her girlhood bedroom, contemplating whether she would ever live on her own again, when the radio exploded with a report she would remember for the rest of her life.

"Attention, America! Attention, America! America is at war! The Japanese have bombed Pearl Harbor! All military back to the base now, no matter where you are or what you're doing. All military people back to the base now!" It had begun.

Lutie Clark was in the hospital at Paintville recuperating from an appendectomy when the time finally came for Jewell and Bryce to seal the promise made on Cypress Hill in Forrest County, Mississippi, more than a year earlier. He had a few weeks of leave before reporting to duty in California. They set the date for June 18, 1942.

Bryce rode in by bus. They gathered all the Clarks together and got married at the Methodist church. Jewell was a lovely bride, and Bryce was a handsome groom in uniform.

After the ceremony and a nice family gathering at the bride's home, the newlyweds hopped the bus back to Lexington accompanied by Burnell, Bryce's baby brother, who'd hitchhiked up from Hattiesburg for the happy event. They got to Lexington, where the couple was spending the night at a hotel close by the depot before taking the train down to Hattiesburg the next morning to see the McMahans. Burnell said good-bye, heading out to find a ride home.

Suddenly, it was about to be the Wedding Night, and the newlyweds began to go through the nervous motions of preparing for the dark.

They went to dinner.

When they returned to the hotel room, Jewell puttered around, turning down covers, making sure everything was straight, neat, packed, unpacked, washed, brushed, and pretty.

She put on her white wedding nightgown and stepped into the bedroom. This was a vision Bryce had waited a long time to see.

Jewell came to the bed.

Bryce reached up, clicked off the light clipped to the top of the headboard, and turned toward his bride.

Knock, knock, knock.

"Who is that? This is a bad time!" the groom growled.

"Let me in! I'm with the wedding party!" a familiar voice boomed from the other side of the door.

It was late and nobody would pick him up, Burnell offered to his glowering brother.

And so the newlyweds and the baby brother spent the honeymoon night sharing a bottle of wine, playing cards, and laughing. Burnell slept a couple of hours on a pallet at the foot of their bed before setting out on the road home again at daybreak.

After seeing Burnell off and bringing his bride a cup of complimentary morning coffee from the lobby, Bryce reminded Jewell they'd soon be leaving.

"Honey, our train leaves at ten o'clock," he said.

"I know."

"Do you want to make that train, or do you want to make love?"

Mr. and Mrs. McMahan took the evening train out of town, bound for Hattiesburg.

THE INCIDENT

Up Home

In February 1959, for the first time in seven months, Ella asked for a Sunday off from her job as head cook at the Hattiesburg Convalescent Center. She and Nelse needed to go see about his sick mother in Noxubee, and Mrs. Mac was happy to grant the leave.

It was daybreak on the fourth Sunday, not long after their twenty-seventh anniversary. Nelse and Ella bustled about their Lee Street home, preparing for the road trip to Shuqualak instead of walking over to Mount Bethel Church. They had received word that Nelse's mother was doing poorly, and so the couple set aside this Sunday for a day trip "up home" to Noxubee County.

Ella had turned forty-six on the Wednesday before, and her children had gifted their mother by singing songs to her, the birthday present she preferred. The sweetest gift to her was the sound of her children's voices. There was no need for a special cake since she always had cake on hand in her kitchen.

February twenty-second was sunny and mild. Dark green daffodil shoots were heralding their coming golden crowns, and the brown grass was crisp over sodden soil. It was a perfect day for a drive.

Across the nation, it was George Washington's 239th birthday, and down in Florida over forty thousand people were filing in to witness the inaugural Daytona 500 race. It would be three days before Lee Petty was declared the winner in the first-ever photo-finish decision. By then, everything would have changed for Ella and Nelse Gaston.

Times were tense in Mississippi. If you were black, it was difficult to keep your children shielded from the dangerous realities of a social system about to explode. Just the previous summer, Samuel Johnson, the fifteen-year-old grandson of a Lee Street neighbor, was shot through the heart by one of two responding white Hattiesburg police officers as he was allegedly trying to burglarize a white residence, according to news reports. The whole affair went away except in the thoughts and prayers of the community and the anguish of his family. Ella and Nelse kept their concerns to themselves whenever the children were around.

Racial tensions were also brewing over Clyde Kennard's repeatedly denied requests to enroll at Mississippi Southern College. A Korean War paratrooper veteran, Kennard had moved back to the Eatonville community in 1955 to help care for his ailing stepfather before finishing his studies at the University of Chicago. Clyde figured the most logical place to complete his degree was the nearby institution. Unfortunately for Clyde, he was black. He was denied admission for three consecutive years. On December 6, 1958, Clyde wrote a lengthy letter subtitled "Mixing" to the editor of the *Hattiesburg American* in which he explained his belief that the integration of the schools was the most pragmatic and effective approach in the expensive undertaking of taxpayer-subsidized education.

A self-described "integrationist by choice," Kennard offered the following as part of the credo of those who had chosen likewise:

> We believe in the dignity and brotherhood of man
> and the divinity and fatherhood of God, and as such,

men should work for the upbuilding of each other, in mutual love and respect. We believe when merit replaces race as a factor in character evaluation, the most heckling social problem of modern times will have been solved.

A few days later, Clyde announced that he would attempt to re-enter the local college, an intent that was well reported. The letter had put him directly in the crosshairs of the state's domestic spying agency, the Mississippi State Sovereignty Commission, which was approached by Hattiesburg lawyer Dudley Conner with an offer to "take care of" the Kennard situation.

On this day, Lee Street was peaceful and pretty, and the family wasn't thinking about the dark, ugly dealings of Southern society. Ella dressed in a simple white blouse and yellow print skirt she'd made herself. Nelse put on a starched blue shirt and khaki pants, ironed lovingly by his daughters. His brown shoes were spit-shined.

Ella and daughter Jean were making sure the younger children were dressed; the fried chicken, pound cake, red rind hoop cheese and crackers were gathered for the trip; and the house was perfectly neat before they stepped out of the door. Ella believed one never left one's house in a mess—who knew what might happen while you were gone, and there you'd be with others seeing what was left behind. Even though the older children were staying in Hattiesburg for the day, you just could never tell. All beds were made, all dishes were done and put away, the bathroom was straightened and freshened up, and the floor was swept. The porch light was on.

Jean, fourteen; Voncile, ten; Michael, six; and Clifford, twelve, were very, very excited. The family eagerly packed up with the four youngest children in the backseat and the food boxes on the floorboard. It was about a three-hour drive, and the youngsters knew they would be spending their time in the car playing games and singing with their mother, a captive playmate.

They were traveling in Nelse's year-old 1958 Ford Fairlane 500 four-door hardtop with a spare on the rear called a Continental Kit. The car was a cool, two-toned green and white model with classic fins and white sidewall tires. Nelse took tender care of it. He was mighty proud to drive it back to the old neighborhood that morning with his beautiful wife in the front seat close beside him and four of their precocious children in the back.

The family pulled away from Lee Street and made their way onto Highway 11 for the trek to Meridian. Ella led them in singing, and they played the ABC game. Starting with *A*, they pointed out words on signs bearing the next alphabet letter. Whoever got to *Z* first won. They could get both a *U* and a *V* on the Burma Shave signs, but they had to be quick to call them first. They would wait for the sign announcing Noxubee County to see who would grab the *X* and *Y* first. There was rarely a *Z*. It was a simple and fun way to pass the time during the long trip up to Shuqualak.

Sometimes they just studied the serene February landscape. In the wintertime, the strong underbrush of the Mississippi woods mostly stood bare, and they could see far away into the trees where the rusty leaf-colored ridges and gullies and old Indian paths wound.

At Meridian, they turned north onto Highway 45, and the children were excited, knowing they'd be on Dorroh Hill Road in a little over an hour.

There was no stopping to go to the bathroom. Public restrooms in Mississippi service stations were reserved for white people only, so the children didn't even ask.

As they pulled into town in Nelse's shiny, showy car, the eyes that watched the comings and goings in Shuqualak made note that there were "uppity" visitors in town.

The Gastons arrived before lunchtime that day. The children piled out to go play with their beloved cousins while their parents stepped inside the modern home that Nelse's sister Jonnie Berniece, or "Jonnie B," and her husband Wallace Lewis had built on the family place. The old three-room house of Nelse's childhood stood abandoned nearby, and his widowed mother was living with his sister's family. His father, "Cap," had died several years before.

Mrs. Annie Slaughter Gaston had been disabled for some time by 1959, though she was able to take a hand in raising her grandson, John. To Nelse, it was important that he offer support and company to his mother and to his sister's family, who sheltered her. The Lewises occasionally made trips down to Hattiesburg too, just to keep the family ties strong.

The Lewis family was self-sufficient in the Dorroh Hill community tradition with a garden plot out back where collards and mustard greens grew in long rows beside stakes tied for the coming runner beans of spring. A hog or two; Old Bessie and Old Nellie, the milk cows; and some chickens all did their part to provide sustenance to the family. Water was still occasionally drawn in a long syrup bucket from a well beside the house, even though they now enjoyed the luxury of indoor plumbing. Out front, Jonnie B planted a catalpa tree in honor of her first daughter's birth so the family would have plenty of live bait for fishing the nearby creeks and streams.

After lunch, the women cleared dishes, and the men moved outside to the front porch where the early afternoon sun was providing a little welcome warmth. The smaller children played on the linoleum floor in the living room while their older siblings tromped through the pastures and woods, enjoying the adventuresome freedom that unfettered nature provides especially for city children.

And then it was time to go. Nelse and Ella began the leaving ritual about two o'clock to ensure daylight travel back home to Hattiesburg. It was dangerous to drive the highways and byways of Mississippi after dark if you were black and in a flashy car. There were multiple good-byes to give and children to convince, and the whole process took on the choreography of a well-rehearsed dance.

The dance extended to the departure ceremony wherein Nelse carefully turned his car around and proceeded down the driveway while the children waved from the backseat and his mother and sister waved back from the front porch. He maneuvered onto the heavily graveled road, moving oh so slowly, so as not to run the risk of chrome or glass being hit by a rock. Nelse next honked ever so slightly at every residence to make sure the entire neighborhood witnessed him driving by in his latest pride and joy. The cousins followed along, running behind the fence line, waving and whooping. It was quite the parade.

The ceremony included Nelse's pulling off the road just beyond the neighborhood so the whole family could pay their respects at the Slaughter Family Cemetery. His mother's people were buried there. Then the Gaston family usually proceeded on out of Shuqualak as quietly as they had arrived.

On this day, as they turned onto Residence Road and made their way past the white people's houses and a lovely old church with a still-intact slave gallery, there appeared to be more activity than usual over in front of Mr. Pete Flora's big white house on Line Street. Nelse could see a Mississippi highway patrol car for one thing. Cautiously, he made a careful right turn onto the paved main thoroughfare. Immediately, red lights popped into his rearview mirror. Nelse carefully pulled as far off the road as he could without hitting Mr. Pete's white picket fence.

"Nelse! What's going on? What's wrong?" Ella asked.

"I don't know," he said, looking in the rearview mirror.

The children, down in the backseat, couldn't see a thing, but they knew better than to insert themselves. Their mama was murmuring, "Quiet, children. Be still." Their daddy kept his eyes glued to the rearview mirror.

All at once, a white man in a gray uniform and swishing a big gun appeared in the window and boomed, "Get out, nigger." Dutifully, Nelse set his jaw and got out of the car.

By this time, three white men in tan uniforms had joined the others. They had arrived sandwiched together in the front seat of a pickup truck.

The children peeped low through the car windows. All they could see were guns, belt buckles, and badges–and Mr. Pete standing in his yard, looking their way, and talking to another big white man in a gray uniform.

Four sets of brown eyes turned their attention to the back of the car. They watched as their daddy was hit in the head so hard that he fell against the trunk, and all of a sudden, the men in tan swarmed him, kicking and cussing and hitting. As one, the children covered their mouths to stifle their screams. They couldn't see their daddy, but they could see the bent figures flailing their arms in the direction of the ground.

Then one of them jerked their daddy up by one arm, spun him around, and put handcuffs on him. He was bleeding. He had a big bump on his head.

The men demanded to know what was in the trunk, took a tire iron from the back of the pickup, tore off the pretty white spare tire, jimmied the trunk open, and stood looking at the empty maw. One of them spit on the ground.

Then Ella said, "Stay still, children," and she got out of the car and went to investigate.

"What you want, nigger?" someone asked her as she approached.

"What's wrong?" she asked. "Why are you arresting my husband?"

"Shut up" was the answer.

Voncile watched in horror as a skinny white man in a tan uniform turned Ella facedown over the trunk and handcuffed her, pressing against her and running his hands all over her.

As Ella and Nelse were led off, Ella looked over her shoulder and shouted to Jean, "Call Hermene! Tell her to call Mrs. Mac!"

The children cried silently while their mama and daddy were pushed into the back of the car with the big writing all over it. Then they were gone–red lights spinning and sirens screaming.

No one in the 1958 Ford Fairlane with the destroyed Continental Kit uttered a word.

We Need a Lawyer

In a little while, one of the younger deputies came over to the car where the terrified Gaston children still sat in a row on the backseat, snuffling tears and staring straight ahead.

"Gal?" he said to Jean. "Can you drive?"

Jean answered, "No, sir," even though she and all three of her siblings knew very well she could. She didn't have a license, though, and she knew that if she attempted to drive off in the car, she may be arrested herself. So she just said no and sat there. She thought, *He was at least kind enough to ask.*

Voncile watched the deputy reach in and grab Ella's purse off the front seat and a long gun out from under the driver seat.

He joined the others on the road behind the car where they examined the weapon, looked in the purse, scratched their heads, and tried to figure out what to do with the children. Nothing, they decided, and the three men in tan uniforms climbed into the pickup truck and sped off to Macon, leaving the damaged Ford Fairlaine and the children right where they were.

As it turned out, someone had passed by the scene and alerted kindly Cousin Nell, Cleo's daughter, who came and got the children.

That night, the children clung to one another in Ella's childhood bed and cried. It was the first night they'd ever spent apart from their mama and daddy. The youngsters stayed the next night at Nell's house too, taking in the comfort of their extended family members and reliving the horrors that had befallen them until Hermene came from Hattiesburg to take them home.

Meanwhile, their parents were spending the night of February 22, 1959, in the lovely, three-story, red brick jailhouse in Macon, which also doubled as the sheriff's residence. Right across from the new courthouse, the jail's charming exterior belied the terror taking place within it. Prisoners were brought up to the second floor from outdoor stairs into the processing room. Once inside the cell block, they could all see the hangman's eyelet and the lever for the gallows on the foursquare walkabout.

Ella had climbed the traditional thirteen steps to the gallows to access her "private cell" on the third floor. It was bare and cold. Looking through classically arched windows only a little obstructed by bars, female prisoners enjoyed a nice treehouse view of Macon. The cell walls were thick but not so thick that the cries of their fellow inmates and the rough twangs of hollering deputies weren't discernable.

For passersby, there wasn't a finer looking building in all of Macon. It was made especially charming by the lacy curtains in the first-floor windows of the sheriff's quarters.

About daybreak on Monday morning, Ella was given a dime and allowed to leave the jail to find a phone to call for help. On her way to the service station, she stepped off the sidewalk to allow a white woman about Hermene's age to pass. It was mighty early for a white woman to be out alone, and it was chilly. Ella's homemade broadcloth shirt wasn't really enough. A light frost sparkled in the sunrise.

Finally at the pay phone, Ella placed a long-distance, collect call to Jewell, who listened, stunned. Ella told her she had been arrested and let out of jail long enough to call for help. If she didn't have someone to bail her out by 9:00 a.m., she'd spend another night in jail. She was sobbing. Nelse was locked up too. Neither one of them knew what for, but she had to get back to the jail. They'd given her thirty minutes to make the call.

Jewell woke Bryce. "Ella's in trouble! We've got to do something!"

Bryce called Attorney Curran W. Sullivan, who placed a call to Jesse P. Stennis, Esquire, of Macon.

Jesse took the daybreak call from Lawyer Sullivan in the kitchen of his modest red brick home on Jefferson Street. Emergency calls at crazy hours weren't all that unusual for the longtime lawyer, who had recently turned criminal defense attorney after years as a prosecutor. His instructions were to 1) go to the jail and find out what happened, 2) make sure Ella Gaston did not spend another night in custody, and 3) do what he could for her husband Nelse.

Curran's law office occupied the second floor of the old Hattiesburg Bank & Trust building on East Front Street, where Bryce had established Beard and McMahan Realty Company. The building's beefy gray marble columns and grand entry were sandwiched between the Owl Drug Store and the Boyd & Caskey Store like an elephant that had stayed too long in one place. Bryce enjoyed the daily challenge of entering his office via an old loading dock ladder out back. Kept him in shape, he said.

Curran reported to his landlords that he'd engaged the best defense attorney for the area, and probably the most expensive lawyer in the district, Jesse Stennis. Curran said he'd meet the McMahans at the office.

Jewell and Bryce scrambled around pulling on clothes, grabbing cups of coffee, and telling their three sons, Lynn, Gary, and Mike, that they were on their own getting to school that day. "Ella's in trouble," they told the startled and sleepy boys as they raced out the door.

The lights were on early at the real estate office on Monday, February 23, and passersby could see the McMahans and the lawyer pacing the floor. They were anxiously waiting for instructions on where to go and what to do next.

Up in Macon, Jesse stepped onto the stoop of the little white building built in 1850 that housed his office. From his post downtown on Jefferson Street, he could take in at one glance the new and majestic two-story Noxubee County courthouse directly across the street, its obligatory lawn decoration—a statue of a Confederate soldier with folded arms—and the lovely red brick jailhouse. Pulling on his jacket and adjusting his tie, Jesse strode over to the home of his longtime acquaintance Emmett W. Farrar Sr., sheriff of Noxubee County. Jesse intended to bail the two prisoners from Hattiesburg out of their overnight quarters with little fanfare.

Jesse was a second cousin of Congressman John C. Stennis from DeKalb, just down Highway 39 in Kemper County. While John went to Washington, Jesse chose to practice law in Noxubee County after serving his country in the Philippines as a Navy officer during World War II. With a law degree from Ole Miss, he was first a county prosecutor and later district attorney, exercising his public service on the same side of the courtroom as Farrar. He had won every time his name appeared on a ballot since he achieved his law degree until the most recent November elections. Jesse had decided to see what the courtroom looked like from the bench and put in a bid to unseat the two-term incumbent circuit court judge John D. Greene Jr. of Oktibbeha County, before whom he had practiced his prosecutorial skills. Judge Greene handed Jesse his first defeat–4,051 to 3,300–and had taken his third oath of office during the first week in January.

Confident he could easily gain the release of the Gastons and find out what all the commotion was about, Jesse stepped into Farrar's domain on the first floor of the jailhouse. The sheriff, on the other hand, was less than happy to see his old comrade.

Heated words were exchanged, and a verbal "rickety" erupted in the residence of the jail. How dare Jesse Stennis question Emmett Farrar on the merits of an arrest? Why, Jesse Stennis had turned into a "nigger lover"! And not only that, he could be arrested himself just for helping the "niggers"!

Jesse retreated to the little white office and placed a call to Lawyer Sullivan.

"What have you all gotten me into?" Jesse demanded of his colleague in Hattiesburg. "They are mad as hell, calling me 'nigger lover' and threatening to arrest me for trying to help these two. This is going to be a tough case; your clients need to know it will be costly. Are they prepared for this?"

"This is going to be expensive," Curran said as he looked at Bryce, who looked at Jewell.

"The sky's the limit," she said.

"Tell him the sky's the limit," Bryce advised.

"The sky's the limit," Curran repeated.

"Well, I'm going after it like a tiger. They won't stop me," the still-smarting defense attorney promised.

And so it was on. Jesse strode purposefully back to the jail. He had the right to know the charges against his clients, and they had the right to get out of jail.

He discovered that Nelse was charged with reckless driving or driving while intoxicated—couldn't tell which—and Ella was charged with either interfering with an officer or intimidating an officer and possession of a concealed weapon. At the moment, the charges were unclear. The sheriff was claiming she'd tried to pull a gun on him.

Begging mercy for a mother whose children needed her, Stennis was successful in persuading the hostile sheriff to release Ella to his personal custody until they could all appear for a bond hearing at the justice of the peace office over in Shuqualak the next day. Nelse stayed in jail.

Having worked closely in the past with Farrar in matters such as these, and well aware of the racially charged proclivities of the sheriff and his gang, Jesse decided to take extra steps to protect his client, a dainty, quiet woman with eyes that watched him imploringly.

The lawmen were inexplicably fractious. So instead of taking her back to Dorroh Hill Road, Jesse took Ella home with him, where Mrs. Stennis was waiting with a hot bath, a hot meal, and a fresh nightgown laid out across the guestroom bed. Ella washed away the dirt and horrors of the night before. She barely touched her lunch, though it was delicious. She called Cousin Cleo to make sure her children were safe. They were better where they were than with her right then. It was a difficult separation, but she stretched out on the bed and slept deeply for the first time since Saturday night.

Meanwhile down in Hattiesburg, the McMahans were gathering papers to secure the Gastons' bonds and preparing for Bryce and Bill

Johnson, Nelse's boss from the meatpacking plant, to make the trip north to Shuqualak on Tuesday for the justice of the peace hearing.

Nelse's sister Jonnie B, a domestic worker for the Floras, also did her part to help. Taking Jean with her, she went to Mr. Pete's big white house and begged Mrs. Flora to help get her family members out of jail.

"They ain't done nothing." Jonnie B stood on the porch and cried through the screen door. "Please help us."

Mrs. Flora said there was nothing she could do, and she closed the door in her housekeeper's face.

Marshal Moore

By Monday afternoon, the *Meridian Star* reported what the commotion was all about: authorities were looking for a black man named Frank Ed Hill of Shuqualak who had pistol-whipped town marshal Ollice Moore in front of Sleepy Hill's store on Saturday night, February 21. Frank Ed was allegedly selling whiskey. He had disappeared after the altercation. Also reported arrested were the suspect's wife, Viola, and his brother, James. Frank Ed was being charged with mayhem.

On Tuesday, the *Vicksburg Post* chimed in that a "Negro couple" had been arrested and were being held in the Noxubee County jail for questioning in relation to the case. All reports detailed that the marshal had sustained scratches to his face and an injured eye. Plus, the "escaped Negro" had taken Moore's service gun and turned it over to Pete Flora for return to its owner.

Oddly, the *Macon Beacon*'s Thursday edition omitted reporting that Pete Flora had wound up with the gun.

Frank Ed Hill, a father of four with one on the way and a much-valued employee of the Shuqualak Lumber Company, was indeed missing. As a matter of fact, he left Noxubee County and Mississippi that night and never returned. Even when his mama passed over forty years later, he didn't come home to Shuqualak. She had told him not to.

His pregnant wife and his brother were in the Noxubee County jail at the same time as his first cousin, Nelse, and his wife, Ella. The Hills had been arrested, hauled in, and beaten in an effort by their captors to locate their quarry, Frank Ed, according to his sister.

This was after Sheriff Farrar and a band of enraged law enforcement officers had kicked in the door of the small, neat white house on Morecock Street in Shuqualak belonging to Alonzo and Pauline Slaughter Hill, Frank Ed's parents. Inside the house that night were five terrified little children, including one who would eventually be the boss of the police department.

Frank Ed's sister, Velma, was ten years old when a nightmare invaded her home. She saw the officers tear into the family's modest possessions—dumping out drawers and cutting through mattresses as though the suspect could be cowering beneath the ticking.

They kept asking Velma's mama for a picture of Frank Ed, and she kept telling them she didn't have any pictures. She didn't take any pictures of her children. She couldn't afford any pictures.

Velma's daddy kept asking the raging uniformed ones why they were tearing up his house. There was no answer except "Shut up."

Alonzo didn't leave that night to try to warn his son. He stayed to help his wife tend to bawling children and clean up the disaster that marauding lawmen had left behind.

Little Velma heard later some of what had happened to Ella and Nelse. It was an awful weekend—just terrible for the Hill family too.

For his part, Frank Ed had made good on his vow that he would never again be taken into the Noxubee County jail and beaten for something he claimed he didn't do, an experience he'd recently undergone.

The Hills were told that Frank Ed and six or seven of his friends were hanging out in the west end of town when Marshal Moore showed up. Moore had been responsible for Frank Ed's lone and memorable trip to lockup a few months previously. The two men began to exchange threatening words, and that was all it took for the marshal. He unholstered his service revolver and approached Frank Ed for an arrest. Frank Ed grabbed the weapon and pistol-whipped the officer with it. Then Frank Ed left the scene on foot, taking the gun with him.

The family suspected that Pete Flora, one of the owners and founders of the Shuqualak Lumber Company and Frank Ed's boss, had helped him escape. Flora was, after all, in possession of the missing gun the next day. It only stood to reason that since he was one of the few people in the area who had the money to pull it off, he could have paid for Frank Ed's transportation out. And, the only way Flora could have had the service weapon was if he had seen Frank Ed after the incident. Nobody else was known to have seen the fugitive.

It was certainly no secret what could happen in Noxubee County to a black man who beat any white man, much less a sworn officer of the law. Five black men had died of suspected lynching in Noxubee County since the turn of the century—and those were the ones people knew about.

The Sheriff and His Men

Narrow faced and wide-shouldered, Emmett W. Farrar Sr. had made quite a reputation for himself as a lawman who kept the "colored problem" well in hand in his neck of the woods. Farrar served as a member of the army's military police during World War II. By 1948, he'd been elected sheriff of his home county, was defeated for a term, and had served seven consecutive years prior to 1959. Farrar, like all other Mississippi sheriffs of the day, was also tax collector. It was a dubious system that was rife with speculation of potential and actual conflicts of interest, and the legislature saw fit to abolish the dual roles in 1972.

Farrar surrounded himself with deputies who emulated his hard-charging style of law enforcement. Odell Hutcherson, one of the officers who had loaded into the front seat of Farrar's truck that February Sunday afternoon to arrest the Gastons, had returned to the force the year before in a most memorable way.

Highway patrolman Charles Staten received a call one early morning from a screaming Marian Farrar begging for help. Her husband, the sheriff, had been wounded; the marshal was hurt; and there was a scuffle at the courthouse. Someone had shown up with a severed human head in his hands.

Hardly believing what he had just heard, Staten rolled out of bed, pulled on his uniform, and headed into town, where he passed Mrs. Farrar transporting the sheriff to the hospital. He could see her horrified face through the windshield.

Once at the courthouse, Staten encountered a bloody scene in the upstairs courtroom that included a battered human head sitting on counsel's podium.

A black man named Alec Bailey, who had been to Whitfield and released about a week prior, had gone missing. Folks were hunting for him. On this particular morning, Roger Stockman had been driving a group of black workers into Macon when they passed Alec walking along Highway 14, headed into town too. He was carrying something. Roger stopped the truck, and Alec climbed aboard. It was then everyone noticed that, besides being clad only in his underwear, Alec was carrying the head of Bull Deale in his hands.

The workers leaped from the back of the truck and fled. Alec stood straight up, holding the head aloft, while Roger creeped his truck into Macon like a grisly parade float and parked on the street between the jail and the courthouse.

Alec waddled into the courthouse. Roger plunged into the jail across the street to alert the sheriff. Farrar and Marshal Wiley Littleton chased Alec up the stairs to the courtroom, where he deposited the gruesome gift. Pulling the fatal pocketknife out of Bull's neck to defend himself against the sheriff and Littleton, Alec inflicted a cut on Farrar from his elbow to his hand. Littleton was stabbed in the side, with the only thing saving him being a rib.

Odell Hutcherson, on a worksite next to the jail when he heard what was happening, ran straight into the melee with a two-by-four, knocking Alec down and finally subduing him with the help of Deputy Cecil Russell. Hutcherson and Russell, described as "much of a man" by Staten, dragged Alec over to the jail and had him hog-tied and in a cell by the time Staten saw him.

Hutcherson was recruited as a deputy shortly thereafter and began serving his second stint as a lawman for the county on February 1, 1958.

Justice of the Peace Court

By Tuesday morning, February 24, Nelse had spent another loud night in the confines of Noxubee County jail with its imposing hangman's décor, the children were still huddled at Cousin Nell's on Dorroh Hill Road, and Ella was picking at a wholesome breakfast of scrambled eggs and bacon at the kitchen table of Jesse and Martha Stennis.

Jesse had told Curran he intended to take on the case "like a tiger," and that was precisely the persona he was adopting.

By extension, the Gaston couple had apparently become targets of the rage law enforcement feels when one of theirs is killed or injured or humiliated. In the highly charged racial environment of the day, a situation where the alleged assailant was black would ensure an even more dramatic reaction.

Constable Moore was still nursing his wounds, inflicted by his own gun at the hands of a black man. And, as further insult to a white man, the Negro wasn't there to take what was coming to him. The accused offender's wife was pregnant and his brother uninformed, so the anger would be visited upon Nelse and Ella, uppity natives who'd made good elsewhere. It was an easy thing to predict.

This is why the rickety had erupted in the jailhouse on Monday morning. This explained the name-calling and social threats levied at Stennis. And it explained why the Stennises had asked Ella if she minded sleeping on the floor underneath the bed the night before, in case someone rode by and fired shots into the bedroom windows.

The tension was tangible.

Not so down in Hattiesburg, where the McMahans, who conducted their business without looking over their shoulders, were busy making sure all paperwork was in order to secure the Gastons' bonds. Forrest County Sheriff Ford Vance was more than happy to sign their bond surety. Bryce and Bill set out at 7:30 a.m. for a 10:30 meeting with Jesse in Macon.

The bond hearing to release Nelse and Ella was scheduled for 2:00 p.m. before Justice of the Peace R. R. (Rufus) Watkins in Shuqualak. Rufus, a rural mail carrier, was also owner of a service station and a nearby taxicab stand in the tiny lumber town. His taxi service offered train passengers transportation to their final destinations and provided Shuqualak residents a way to get to Brooksville, Macon, and sometimes even Columbus. Ladies whose husbands did all the driving occasionally needed a ride. Justice of the Peace Watkins was an entrepreneurial fellow.

In Mississippi, the office of justice of the peace was created in the originating state constitution of 1817. Modeled after judicial practices of medieval England, justices were assigned jurisdiction over both civil and criminal proceedings as almost a neighborhood convenience. They presided over the court of first resort in matters of misdemeanor criminal charges and were often the court of last resort for minor civil disputes. There was no requirement of degree or training. Just being a white male and able to win an appointment or a popular election was enough to put a person on the bench in a Mississippi justice of the peace court. The courts were informal institutions where justices often heard cases in offices located in their homes or outbuildings in their yards.

Record keeping at the justice of the peace level was haphazard at best. For cases proceeding to a circuit court or to a grand jury, what usually followed the defendant were the order and a bond notice. Justices kept their court record proceedings as they pleased, and there was no standardized procedure in place to ensure continuity of a court record.

Jesse's clients intended to take this case as far as necessary to make sure that Ella Gaston would never be incarcerated again. For that goal, a reliable testimony record was necessary.

So Jesse took the remarkable step of engaging a court reporter to take down the justice of the peace proceedings after this bond hearing. It was an expensive but essential move to preserve testimony that could be called upon in the future. Harpole Patterson of Eupora, Fourteenth Chancery Court District Court Reporter, was enlisted for the job. As it turned out, hiring a court reporter was one of the most inspired decisions that Jesse Stennis made on behalf of Ella Gaston.

Jesse waited in his neat little white office on Jefferson Street, where he was supposed to meet Bryce and Bill. They were bringing Jesse's retainer and documents to secure bonds for Nelse and Ella. Pulling into town after a three-hour drive from Hattiesburg, the visitors' arrival was noted from a first-floor window of the jail across the way.

About the time introductions were being made, the office phone rang. It was the sheriff, informing Jesse that Nelse Gaston couldn't be released without proper identification. It seemed he'd been unable to locate an "official" copy of his driver's license since they first pulled him over in Shuqualak. Too bad the fellas had made a trip all the way up from Hattiesburg. Nelse Gaston wasn't going anywhere.

Jesse relayed the time-sensitive message.

"We'll see about that," Bryce said as he asked to use the phone.

The others heard only one side of the conversation.

"Honey," he said, "they're saying Nelse doesn't have a driver's license."

"Yeah. You're going to have to go get an official copy of his application from the highway patrol office at the courthouse. It's gotta be up here by two o'clock."

"Yes, that's what I said—by two o'clock," he repeated.

"Yes. I know if anybody can do it, you can."

"Be careful and don't get caught."

Bryce put down the receiver and looked at the two men.

"She'll be here," he said. "Don't worry about it."

Stennis would soon find out who "she" was.

In Hattiesburg, Jewell checked her watch. She had a little over three hours to get the license and arrive on time at justice court in Shuqualak. She called the highway patrol office and told the receptionist she was on her way to get a copy of Nelse Gaston's driver's license application and not to ask questions. It was an emergency.

Jumping into her black Lincoln, Jewell sped away from the nursing home parking lot and over to Forrest County Courthouse on North Main Street downtown. As expected, the lady at the highway patrol desk had the application copy waiting for Jewell.

Leaving Hattiesburg with the document in hand, Jewell never looked back, and she never looked down at the speedometer, except once.

"It was going pretty fast, but then that Lincoln would run," she finally admitted fifty-one years later.

Going to Court

In Macon, as she dressed for her debut in her role as criminal defendant, Ella wondered how she had wound up at this place, in the house of strange white people, away from her children for the first time in their lives, preparing to be tried as someone who had intimidated a white sheriff—the notorious Emmett Farrar, no less.

Dressed in a wig, hat, dark glasses, and Mrs. Stennis's dress, Ella cautiously stepped onto the Stennis's back carport, where Jesse was holding the back door of his sedan open for her. She was used to riding in backseats of white people's cars; it was an excuse to be pulled over to do otherwise. After all, black and white people riding as equals were a cause for alarm throughout the Mississippi countryside. Ella also would be lying on the floorboard to escape notice of those in Macon who would be watching the comings and goings of the driver, her lawyer. As an extra precaution, Mrs. Stennis had been invited along for the ride south to Shuqualak.

There was no doubt this could turn ugly. Jesse was not a small man, and his English language command could usually overtake the most belligerent redneck, but this was different. They'd be facing a force of armed officers who had worked themselves into a self-righteous fury aimed straight at his client.

Gravel

It was a simple bond hearing—simple, regular justice of the peace business. Except this time, it was different, Rufus Watkins admitted to himself.

The hearing could become a full-blown circus. Anybody who'd ventured out of his or her front door in Shuqualak since Saturday night had been subjected to tales of Marshal Moore's beating. Additionally, the Watkins family was in an uproar. Ollice Moore was Rufus Watkins's son-in-law.

The "Negro couple's" arrest out in front of Pete Flora's house during a pleasant Sunday afternoon drive time guaranteed that the story developed even more hyperbole. The car alone was enough to create a sensation.

Shuqualak was full of it. And so Rufus decided to hold the hearing at Shuqualak City Hall, which was graced with a gravel parking lot and more room than his home or other justice of the peace court settings. Rufus was running for reelection after a little over three years of service. The outcome of this hearing could matter to the outcome of his reelection bid.

First in the courtroom were Nelse Gaston and a deputy. Nelse was cuffed and manacled and looked like he'd spent the last few nights sleeping on a floor somewhere; he probably had, depending on how crowded the county jail had been. A closer look revealed a nice pair of shoes and good clothes—wrinkled and dirty, but quality.

Nelse was deposited on the bench reserved for the accused, and the lawman who brought him dashed outside to stand guard. A few more than the usual regular court crowd wandered in, taking their seats along the back of the room. Clad in overalls and plaid shirts, a few in khakis, most of the men were farmers. All were white. The men in khakis sat to themselves and didn't have much to say.

There was very little real entertainment in Shuqualak, and this situation was definitely the hottest thing going. Planting season was a ways off.

Gravel popping outside heralded the arrival of multiple vehicles. It wasn't going to be a fun afternoon at all, but Rufus had a plan to transfer this monkey off his back. He had an order ready to let the elderly and experienced T. E. Woodfin, his justice of the peace partner in District 4, take care of it. With Ollice's being potentially involved in the case, Rufus felt that a change of venue was in order. His counterpart would get the honors.

Among those entering the courtroom was District Attorney H. T. Carter, who had left the courthouse in Macon for this occasion. It was an election year, and Carter wanted to make sure he was seen doing his job, even if he did have to leave the Grand Jury in full swing. This thing had made the newspapers, and Carter needed to be here. He'd been challenged by young Harvey S. Buck from over at West Point first thing out of the box in January, and even though Carter was the incumbent, he knew Buck was going to give him a run.

By February 24, 1959, the idea of Mississippi's hard-won, segregated societal order being overturned was a very scary and very real proposition for many white people. This thing with the "Negroes" and the marshal was serious. Everyone was watching.

In strode Emmett Farrar. His wife, Marian, had announced the week prior that she'd be running for sheriff, but her victory would ensure that Emmett would continue to be the man in charge. He'd served two consecutive terms, which was the statutory limit for service. They'd decided Marian could be his placeholder since he couldn't run for reelection. It was a common practice in Mississippi. Farrar took his seat up front beside the justice of the peace, where he'd be bailiff for the proceeding. It gave the sheriff a great face-to-face opportunity to stare down defendants and their attorneys.

Farrar certainly had a reputation as a very dangerous man, Jewell had learned. Jesse had warned them that Farrar was a "mean son-of-a-gun" and he "ruled the roost up there."

Around 1:50 p.m., Jesse and his female passengers arrived at court. Their welcoming party was a wall of uniformed white men displaying the classic dominant male pose, with hands on hips and flat fingers pointing in the direction of their crotches. Guns and badges were glinting in the sunshine. In the parking lot, Bryce and Bill had been sitting in their sedan waiting for backup.

They all crunched their way through the rocky parking lot to get to the door.

Tall and broad, Jesse's was a commanding figure as he entered the building. He carried a worn leather briefcase in one hand. His other hand was on the back of the second defendant, Ella Gaston. Modestly dressed and a pretty woman by any standard, she didn't take her eyes off her husband as Stennis helped her to her place on the bench. The couple didn't speak, but they joined hands around his handcuffs and turned their attention to the floor.

Mrs. Stennis found a seat away from a boorish group of spectators who'd reduced their remarks to side-mouthed one-liners. She kept her purse firmly in her lap.

The men from Hattiesburg entered. Both visitors wore the best suits that Fine Brothers Matison had to offer—crisp dress shirts, silk ties, and shined shoes. One of them was particularly notable. Thick and tall, he carried himself like a man who wasn't used to losing a fight. One look at his hands destroyed any question on the matter; they were as big as catcher's mitts. The out-of-towners went over to the Gastons and patted their shoulders. All four engaged in classic motions of empathy as they nodded and shook their heads together in sorrow at the circumstances in which they found themselves. The big guy checked his watch and inspected folded papers stored in the inside pocket of his suit jacket. He was the picture of composure.

The sheriff smugly observed the highfalutin' pair. What a wasted trip they'd made. Gaston wasn't going anywhere. He had no driver's license. Heck, the man couldn't even prove who he was.

Marshal Moore gingerly made his way in. He had a busted lip and patched eye, and he moved very slowly. The locals looked anywhere but at him, embarrassed. *It was bad enough to get beat up by a darkie*, they were thinking, *much less with your own gun.*

R. L. Richardson, the highway patrolman who'd ordered Nelse out of the car, came in and took a seat. He wasn't looking to the right or to the left. Neither was his partner, Charles Staten, who joined him.

Well, looks like everybody's here, Rufus thought, looking at his watch. It wasn't quite two o'clock. "Might as well get started," he ventured.

No sooner had he said it than the spectators jumped at startling sounds of tires slinging into gravel.

Jewell McMahan had made it to court on two wheels and with two minutes to spare. She was grabbing the license, her gun, and her purse when the skinny deputy recovered himself enough to run over to the Lincoln and yell through the window at her.

"You can't drive up in here like that!"

"I just did."

"You can't take that gun in there!"

"Watch me," she replied as she put her sidearm in her purse and paced off the four strides it took to get inside the building.

"You know," Jewell told Bryce later, "that gravel parking lot ruined a perfectly good pair of heels."

Suddenly, the smartly dressed, dark-haired businesswoman was in command of everyone's attention inside. Jewell nodded crisply to the stunned locals, walked over to Rufus's desk, planted a piece of paper in front of him, and turned her face to the sheriff.

"Judge, I believe you may need this today," the woman said in the officer's direction. "It's Nelse Gaston's driver's license application." She turned a radiant smile to the judge.

Jewell strolled over to the defendants, hugged Ella, patted Nelse on the knee, and took her seat beside the beaming visitors from Hattiesburg.

Farrar didn't flinch. The man with the big hands smiled broadly as he turned over his papers to his lawyer. Jesse Stennis buttoned his suit jacket as he stood up.

The driver's license application's arrival ensured that the proceeding would be a going-through of motions. Prosecutors took a moment to present charges, and Jesse made remarks on behalf of his clients.

Soon enough, it was over. Ella and Nelse would be in justice of the peace court again on March 27, but then they would appear before somebody else. Rufus announced his intent to transfer the case to Justice of the Peace Woodfin.

Bryce and Bill provided documentation from Forrest County to prove there was enough financial wherewithal standing by in Hattiesburg to pay the bond for Ella and Nelse, in case the two decided to run away between now and their justice of the peace court appearance in March. The bond security included Bryce and Jewell's house.

Nelse and Ella were going home.

The officers filed out, and the State gathered up papers for a quick trip back over to Macon. The District 16 prosecution lineup was spread pretty thin at the courthouse because of this hearing. Circuit court was in full operation.

Out on the gravel, the defense team shook hands all around. Bill said he'd be happy to drive Nelse and Ella home to Hattiesburg. Mrs. Stennis handed Ella a little bag with her homemade clothes inside.

There was one more thing.

Tall and thin, the sheriff swaggered about, showing off his guns, making sure onlookers knew he was in charge. To Jewell, he looked like a thug.

"Hey, Sheriff!" Jewell shouted to Farrar across the parking lot. "These two will never serve a day–ever."

"You need to stay out of Sheriff's business with the niggers!" he shouted back.

"See ya in court," she said with a smile as she got into the Lincoln's shotgun seat.

Bryce and Jewell stopped off in Meridian at the Red Hot Truck Stop for a cup of coffee and a sandwich.

"So just how fast were you going?" Bryce cautiously asked.

"Fast enough to get there on time," she answered.

It was the last time he ever inquired.

This day's adventure to the justice of the peace office set roles played out by the Gaston team over the case's entire course. Ella would be the reserved and graceful sympathetic character; Jewell would be her resourceful and fearless sidekick; Jesse would be the crafty and towering intellectual tiger; Bryce would be the solid and steady defender; and Nelse would be the elegant and handsome, ever-faithful spouse, willing to sacrifice his own pride to protect the love of his life.

Acting Normal

A last thing Jewell had said to Ella when they took their separate ways from Shuqualak was "Don't worry about coming in for the rest of this week. We'll talk about it later."

The Gastons' eldest daughter, Hermene, had picked up her four youngest siblings from Cousin Nell's and had driven them back to Hattiesburg the morning of the hearing.

Back on Lee Street, Nelse and Ella were welcomed home by their squealing and sobbing children. Michael put his arms around his mama's legs and hung on while his sisters and brothers mobbed their parents. The churchwomen had brought big food, and Hermene bustled around in the kitchen, getting everything ready for a homecoming meal. The family gathered around the table, held hands, and praised God for this moment.

When questions came about where they'd been and what the police had done to them, the parents deftly switched the subject to something more enjoyable, like asking the children what they had done during their extra two days on Dorroh Hill Road.

Lying in their bed that night, Ella and Nelse held hands and stared at the ceiling of the bedroom Nelse had built with his own two hands. It had been terrible, just terrible. Too bad to talk about. They determined they would never mention it in front of their children—ever.

Nelse got up the next morning and pulled on his starched and pressed work clothes. He polished his Stacy Adams shoes and set them back in the closet where they belonged. They were a little scuffed from the ordeal, but several shinings should eventually wipe away the remnants of two nights in the Noxubee County jail.

Ella was already up fixing breakfast and getting the children off to school. She was going through morning motions so familiar to everyone—preparing a big breakfast of grits, eggs, bacon, homemade biscuits, and orange juice in little glasses with yellow, orange, and red painted stripes on them. Like always, she cooked enough to feed her family and whoever else wandered in to wait for the school bus and looked hungry.

Everyone was eventually gone. Ella was alone. She sat still on the couch in her quiet living room and contemplated what was ahead of her. There would be another court appearance in another mean, crowded room—that much she knew for sure. Jesse had said they would probably end up going all the way to the circuit court in the big new courthouse across from the jail, probably even farther than that.

She'd never paid a lot of attention to how courts and such things worked. It just wasn't something women in the South did, white or black. They didn't go to jail. They didn't go to court. It was unseemly. And besides, except for an assistant or a reporter or a maid, there was really no reason for a woman to be in a courtroom. They couldn't serve on juries, and there were precious few female lawyers in Mississippi. And here she was accused of a crime. She had been thrown into the back of a highway patrol car in handcuffs and in front of her children. She'd spent a night under arrest. It was just too much.

Ella drew the curtains and sat in the early morning shadows.

Jewell arrived at the Hattiesburg Convalescent Center early on Wednesday morning. Her employees were busy making sure everything was just so for her arrival. Everyone knew Ella had troubles. Exactly what they were was a mystery, but word traveled. They all knew Mrs. Mac had torn out of the office the day before to take something to Nelse and Ella in Shuqualak.

Jewell greeted everyone by name and stopped to inspect a couple of client rooms. She spot-checked every day to make sure rooms and bathrooms were clean and patients were ready to take on the day, whatever *ready* meant to them as individuals. All of her charges must be bathed and completely dressed every single day. Each female client must have her hair done and her lipstick on, every day. No excuses. It gave residents hope and purpose, Jewell believed.

She reported to the kitchen that Ella would be gone for several days but that she was back in Hattiesburg and doing just fine. Then Jewell went to her office and closed the door. This was going to be a long haul, but she was going to make good on her promise. Ella Gaston would never spend another night in jail, ever. Ella was her employee, true, but she was also her friend.

•

The State of the State

In the month or so between the bond hearing and the justice of the peace trial set for March 27 in T. E. Woodfin's court, Bryce made a couple of trips to Noxubee County. The first was to take Nelse up home to retrieve his beat-up Fairlane 500. Bryce was glad to go because he wanted to ask a few questions from folks in the Dorroh Hill community and elsewhere in Noxubee. Specifically, he wanted to find out everything he could about law enforcement, Noxubee County style.

Things were extraordinarily bad all over Mississippi for black people who were accused of crimes, or not, and Noxubee seemed to be a case study in discrimination. Bryce found segregation in the extreme in the rural county that had once harbored the whole of Mississippi state government. Blacks certainly couldn't use the same restrooms as whites; they had to enter businesses and homes through the back door; eating at the same table with whites was unheard of; and failing to yield right of way on the sidewalk or on the road could be downright dangerous.

If you put all of this under the cold scrutiny of fresh eyes, anybody should see that this way of living was just crazy.

What Bryce found in the Dorroh Hill community was a surprisingly self-contained society, inhabited by kind but very cautious people. Apparently, most white men who visited weren't on friendly missions.

Even as shocking as things were in Noxubee, Forrest County wasn't exactly an exemplary model of progressive race relations either, though the McMahans' own experiences with black people there had been friendly and mutually respectful. It appeared that way to Jewell and Bryce, at least. Hattiesburg was beginning to hear the rumblings of racial tensions that the McMahans were seeing in Noxubee. Of course, looking at things through a white man's eyes often yielded a picture much different than others'. This much Bryce knew.

The 1954 *Brown v. Board of Education* decision had created an effective race war conducted on the subject of school integration in South Mississippi, including emboldened public stances on both sides of the issue. Bryce had a ringside seat in the education arena as a local school board member. In Hattiesburg, at least, the board could honestly say that black and white school buildings were now built to the same codes and all teachers were paid the same. Bryce had insisted. The system wasn't perfect, he knew, but it was at least decent—comparatively speaking.

Hattiesburg had been rocked in December by the plainspoken Clyde Kennard letter to the editor of the *Hattiesburg American* calling for integration of the schools. Some city "fathers" were even making plans to take Kennard out of the discussion altogether, or so Bryce had heard. There was no telling what would actually happen.

Add to the seething mix the fact that it was an election year, and the racist rhetoric seemingly knew no bounds. Segregation and keeping the black population in its place while preserving Mississippi's Jim Crow society comprised the most popular theme among all white candidates in 1959—from constable to governor.

A Piney Woods neighbor and two-term lieutenant governor, Carroll Gartin of Laurel, was launching a campaign for governor, from which office he intended to enforce strict segregation of the races. Gartin and Jesse Stennis had both attended the 1956 Democratic Convention. Gartin was a delegate; Stennis, an alternate. Gartin was considered the "moderate" in the gubernatorial race, compared to demagogue Ross Robert Barnett, who at sixty-one was a two-time loser in his previous bids for the governorship.

Whereas Gartin's campaign rhetoric bordered on bland ("I have said, and I repeat now, that Mississippi faces two paramount problems; the first is successful maintenance of segregation, and the second is continued economic progress"), Barnett's announcement dramatically laid out the white voting majority's agenda for the campaign season:

I am a vigorous segregationist. I will work to maintain our heritage, our customs, constitutional government, rights of the states, segregation of the races, and industrial and agricultural development. The next governor will be confronted with some of the most complicated problems since the era of Reconstruction, following the War Between the States. I owe allegiance only to my God, my family, my conscience, and the good people of my native state.

Former district attorney Charlie Sullivan of Clarksdale was also running, but his platform was curious for the venue—he was calling for legalization of alcoholic beverages. In a Southern Baptist stronghold state, the idea was clearly out of kilter. Few would publicly proclaim they were actually in favor of legalized liquor. Sullivan's campaign appeared doomed, not only by the teetotaler Baptists but also by those whose livelihood was dependent upon the illegality of alcohol. And there were quite a number of those.

A chief duty of the state office of tax collector was to make sure that all alcohol was adequately levied for taxes, illegal or not. William F. Winter, thirty-six, of Grenada had announced his candidacy for the post. He was currently filling the unexpired term of the widow of the former governor, Mrs. Thomas C. Bailey, who had died in office in 1956 after serving since 1947. Most purveyors of both imported and "domestic" alcohol didn't mind paying the taxes to stay in the lucrative business.

Sullivan's creative, though disconnected, platform, and the fact that Gartin had made the mistake of challenging Big Jim Eastland in his 1954 Senatorial reelection bid, would eventually help ensure that

Mississippi's next leader would be the Jackson trial lawyer with the fire-and-brimstone demeanor of an old-time preacher–Ross Barnett.

Paul B. Johnson Jr., son of Forrest County's sole gubernatorial product, and a lawyer himself, was on the Democratic ticket for lieutenant governor. He had tried three times previously to repeat his father's trip to the governor's mansion and failed.

Theron Lynd, a Hattiesburg business owner, had announced he was running for Forrest County circuit clerk, the elected front line of defending Mississippi's polling places from the dreaded "Negro vote."

In Noxubee, the district attorney whose office was prosecuting Ella and Nelse was in a fight for his seat after only one term.

H. T. Carter had been challenged by Harvey Buck, a young lawyer from West Point. While one would think Buck, at age thirty-seven and barely out of law school, was hardly a serious contender, he was a savvy politician who was making sure that voters, who were almost without exception white, knew exactly where his priorities lay. "To the White Democratic Voters of Noxubee County," his January 15 appeal in the *Macon Beacon* had started, "If you will elect me your District Attorney, I pledge to devote the full power of the office and of my ability as a lawyer to a full and complete enforcement of all of the criminal laws of our state and to preserving our segregated society and public schools, during my term."

Not to be out "white-supremacied," in February, Carter had also addressed his announcement "To the White Voters." He went a step further and mentioned outside "agitators" who were stirring up the races and claimed that the 1959 election was coming at a "crucial" time in the state's history. He asked voters to give him an "endorsement term" of a second four years.

Both men were Shriners and Masons, with Carter holding the thirty-third degree. Both were, of course, Democrats. Ever since the bloody and violent overthrow of Reconstruction in Mississippi during the 1874 election, essentially only one race voted for candidates of only one party–and it wasn't the GOP.

The solidly conservative Mississippi Democratic Party of 1959 was, for all purposes, the only party in the state, completely overshadowing the overwhelmed Republicans' feeble efforts. The Mississippi Democratic Party had been born in reaction to the Reconstruction specter of freed slaves actually holding elected offices throughout the state and also voting, and, eighty-four years later, the party was holding on to its hard-won entitlement. So its 1959 candidates were not at all bashful about claiming the bloody inheritance that had put their party in power.

It was against this ever-sharpening, bitter backdrop that Nelse's and Ella's lives and livelihoods came to be at the mercy of Noxubee County officials whose oaths of office were as much to the "Southern Way of Life" as to the constitutions of the United States and Mississippi.

During the second trip to Noxubee, Bryce and Bill brought another payment for Jesse and reconnoitered the lay of the land, trying to make connections with some local white people who might give them a different perspective on how justice was conducted in Noxubee. Not surprisingly, they didn't find out much from the white citizenry.

They met with Jesse in the little white building, where he explained the trial strategy he intended to employ and warned them that there would be more court appearances to come. His objective was to get the case before the state Supreme Court. The defense crew all reckoned that their deliberate nose-thumbing at the Noxubee establishment would be costly and drawn out, but they all were determined that neither Ella nor Nelse would be incarcerated in Noxubee County ever again.

When the group met again, it was for the justice court hearing before T. E. Woodfin in Macon. Jesse told them it would be simply a *pro forma* exercise. There was little doubt that both Nelse, who was variously charged with drunk driving and reckless driving, and Ella, who was charged with either disorderly conduct or intimidating a police officer or interfering with an officer as well as carrying a concealed weapon, would be found guilty by the justice of the peace. Charges against the two were never really well defined, a typical treatment of black offenders in the day.

For appeal purposes, Jesse said the best he could hope for would be discrepancies in testimony from the justice of the peace court to the circuit court. The only way to prove it was with a hearing transcript. It was good that Harpole Patterson had agreed to take on the job of paid court reporter for the defense. Harpole lived in Winston County and likely wouldn't be as intimidated by the prospect of having to face the Noxubee gang daily. He'd accepted the job, but he wasn't cheap.

Ella Gaston, age thirty, 1943

The dapper Nelse Gaston outside Mount Bethel Baptist Church, 1976

Ella and Nelse Gaston observing their fiftieth wedding anniversary.

The Gaston family in their Lee Street home: (standing, from left) Leuvell, Voncile, Jean, Juanita, and Michael; (seated, from left) Clifford, Ella, Nelse, and Hermene, early 1970s

Ella Gaston inside Mount Bethel Baptist Church in 1976

Jewell Clark (McMahan) as a student at Bowling Green Business College

Bryce McMahan as a student at Mississippi Southern College

BOXING

First Row: Robert Corrales, Bill Weaver, James Palencia, Arthur Wood, Jack Cook.

Second Row: Bud Lewis, Victor Royal, Bryce McMahan, R. L. McArthur, Dallas Smith, James Hopper, Mgr.

The boxing team closed a very successful season this year with victories in four of their six matches. Although many new faces appeared on the squad all proved to be seasoned boxers. Coach Lewis did an excellent job of coaching, developing four state champions. Captain McMahan concluded his two years of boxing undefeated, winning eight bouts and drawing two, and climaxing his career with the state championship.

Arthur Wood sustained an injury to his arm early in the season which forced his withdrawal from the squad.

Robert Corrales won the state championship in the bantamweight division, being victorious in three bouts and losing one.

Victor Royal, although with little ring experience, came through with a good record in the Bulldog squad.

R. L. McArthur scored a number of knockouts, climaxing the season by winning the state championship.

Jack Cook, freckled-faced, red-headed Texan, turned in a fine record until he sustained an eye injury which stopped his rapid progress.

Bill Weaver, tough coast battler, fought his way into the hearts of Perk's ring fans. He deserves recognition as one of the gamest fighters in Bulldog history.

James Palencia, after a slow start, came into his own in the middle of the season to do himself and Perkinston credit.

Dallas (Cannonball) Smith, middleweight champion, turned in the squad's best record with five victories and one draw.

Bryce McMahan touted as heavyweight boxing champion of Mississippi in the Perkinston Junior College yearbook

101

FCAHS faculty lineup for fall semester, 1940, with Jewell
Clark (McMahan) second from left in the front row

The McMahan boys (from left), Gary, Mike, and Lynn, 1958

The Noxubee County Courthouse

The Noxubee County Library (former jail), exterior

Interior of the Noxubee County Library with
hangman's eyelet still attached to the ceiling

Ella's daughters Voncille (left) and Jean with Jewell McMahan 2011

Co-conspirators Mike McMahan and "Esta" Harris, 2012

Good Friday

March 27, 1959, was Good Friday.

Instead of preparing for a big Easter Sunday celebration at Mount Bethel Church in Hattiesburg, Nelse and Ella were on their way to stand trial as criminal defendants in their home county. Azaleas, dogwoods, and wisteria vines were putting on an Easter parade across the spring green countryside speeding past the car windows, the couple observed from the backseat of the McMahan car. It was as sad a day as they'd ever spent.

The defendants Gaston had ridden up with Bryce and Bill in Jewell's Lincoln. Its parking lot arrival on this day wasn't nearly as spectacular as it had been the month before; Jewell had stayed in Hattiesburg on nursing home business. Woodfin's justice of the peace court was in the little white building next door to the courthouse in Macon.

Jesse welcomed the Hattiesburg contingent into the small courtroom. Ella and Nelse took the defendants' seats. Nelse didn't bear the shameful chains he had worn before. Ella wore a demure skirt and blouse. He wore khakis and a blue shirt, and his Stacy Adams shoes were shined this time.

On this court day, most farmers were out tending their places. Whether or not it came as a memorial to Jesus Christ, crucified and entombed on this day in Christianity's most important act of selflessness, Good Friday was considered the prime day for planting in Mississippi. It was especially so in Noxubee County's agrarian culture.

In his midseventies, Thomas Edward Woodfin was a veteran of the bench. A resident of Mushulaville, Woodfin was the sheriff's distant cousin and had been a justice of the peace for a very long time. He had apparently lost count of how long he'd served; his reelection announcement in the March 12 *Macon Beacon* merely said he'd been serving a "number of years." He had been conducting marriage ceremonies at least as far back as 1929.

Woodfin's co-justice of the peace for the Fourth District, Rufus Watkins, had asked voters to give him a second term via the March 5 edition of the weekly newspaper. Watkins had gotten out of this Gaston situation quite handily, Woodfin thought.

The state was represented by District Attorney Carter, who remained unwavering in his goal to demonstrate to the good, law-abiding white citizens of Shuqualak that he would keep the "Negro problem" under control during his watch.

The primary charge against Ella, as sworn to on February 24 by Emmett Farrar and later filed on April 21, 1959, in circuit court for Cause No. 3644, was read aloud:

> [Ella Gaston] did willfully and unlawfully attempt to impede and intimidate Emmett W. Farrar, the duly qualified and acting Sheriff of Noxubee County, Mississippi, in the discharge of the duty of said Emmett W. Farrar as such Sheriff, by approaching said Sheriff with a woman's handbag containing a pistol and opening said bag and stating to the said Sheriff 'you cannot arrest my husband', when he the said Sheriff was legally arresting one, Nelse Gaston, husband of said Ella Gaston for the crime of driving an automobile while under the influence of intoxicating liquor against the peace and dignity of the State of Mississippi.

The prosecution presented its case.

After the usual introductions and declarations, the sheriff was sworn to tell the truth and nothing but. Farrar then told the story of how he and other officers had spoken with Nelse on the morning of February 22 to see if he knew anything about Frank Ed Hill. Then the sheriff testified that he and other officers had observed Nelse taking off and throwing gravel in their direction on Dorroh Hill Road. Then he'd radioed highway patrolmen to stop the Gaston car. And when he and his two deputies arrived in the sheriff's pickup at the stopped vehicle site, he had arrested Nelse, who was already out of the car and looking for his driver's license, thanks to Patrolman Richardson. Farrar also testified that nobody hit Nelse and that Ella had approached the sheriff with her purse, but she had neither opened nor reached into it.

Deputy W. O. Hutcherson also took the stand. He testified that Farrar told Nelse he was being arrested for reckless driving. He recalled that Ella had unsnapped her purse and had reached her hand into it as she was coming around behind the car to protest her husband's arrest. He also said he told Nelse to raise his hands because he was under arrest and that Nelse had laughed at him. Hutcherson testified that after Nelse laughed at him, he hit Nelse to get him to raise his hands for cuffing once the sheriff pronounced Nelse under arrest.

During the interim month, highway patrolman Richardson had resigned his post and returned home to Louisville, where he was owner and operator of a dry-cleaning and laundry business. Nevertheless, he was present in justice court and testified that Farrar had snatched Ella's purse away from her, reached inside it, and pulled out a gun. Richardson had not seen her open or unsnap it.

Also in the witness seat was Allen Lanier, who had been sworn as a special deputy for the manhunt following Ollice Moore's beating. The aspiring lawman was a Macon contractor who had just announced his candidacy for constable of District 3 against incumbent James Jernigan.

All officers seemed to have had trouble counting the "darkies" in the Gastons' backseat; the count varied from five to eight, depending on who was talking.

The defense called no witnesses.

As expected, Judge Woodfin found Ella guilty of obstructing justice and ordered her to pay a fine of twenty-five dollars and serve sixty days in the county jail at hard labor. Immediately, Jesse entered an appeal to circuit court and produced an appeal bond guaranteed by Mr. and Mrs. G. W. (Bill) Causey and fellow Hattiesburg businessman Gordon Hicks in the amount of two hundred dollars. The bond stated that Ella had been found guilty of intimidating an officer. The amount was certified by Forrest County Sheriff Vance and approved by Judge Woodfin.

The concealed weapon charge against Ella was determined valid and an appropriate fine affixed. It too was appealed.

Nelse was undramatically found guilty of driving while under the influence of intoxicating liquor. Bond was posted with the McMahans' home listed as collateral, and, like Ella's, his case was pressed on to circuit court.

Everything had happened just about like the Gastons, McMahans, Johnson, and their lawyer had figured it would.

Jesse's decision to hire Harpole Patterson to record the proceedings would prove most fortunate. Already, the officers' testimonies had gaping inconsistencies. No telling what it would be like in circuit court.

Everyone packed up and went their separate ways, preparing to go through it all again during the August term of circuit court.

The Lincoln headed south toward Hattiesburg. To pass the time, its occupants traded observations about characters they'd encountered in court that day. To be sure, the backwoods accents and court players' language had been entertaining. It was always better to laugh than cry, and it helped dispel the cloud of August following them home.

Once back on Lee Street, Nelse and Ella greeted their children with smiles and hugs, and everyone talked excitedly about the big egg dyeing and cooking coming the next day in preparation for Easter Sunday. Ham, deviled eggs, macaroni and hoop cheese, and coconut cake were on the menu. The girls were excited about wearing their mother's latest designs to church, and the boys were planning the best hiding places for bright eggs dyed with vinegar and food coloring.

Easter was always a joyous occasion in the Gaston household.

The Darkening Days of Summer

Between the March 27 hearing in Judge Woodfin's courtroom and the August circuit court trial date, Mississippians were sweltering in one of the hottest summers on record. But if weather was hot, the campaign rhetoric was hotter.

The summer's political pandering was confined nearly exclusively to one topic–keeping black people "in their places." Almost without exception, each white Democratic candidate was eager to paint himself (rarely herself) as more segregationist than the opponent.

Gubernatorial frontrunner Barnett went so far as to describe black citizens of his state thusly: "The Negro is different because God made him different to punish him. His forehead slants back. His nose is different. His lips are different, and his color is sure different," according to *Time* Magazine's campaign coverage.

His opponent, Gartin, ran half-page ads in the July 15 Mississippi newspapers elevating his segregationist stand: "Carroll Gartin is dedicated, determined, and pledged to total segregation! ... I shall never weaken in my stand for complete segregation. No hardships will be too great for me to endure personally and as governor of Mississippi in my stand for segregation."

Lieutenant governor hopeful Johnson bought newspaper advertisements declaring, "The proven price of racial integration is the enormous skeleton of dead empires. I have been, and now and always will be, dedicated by determined action, to maintain the segregated ways of our people that make for continued peace and prosperity."

For black Mississippians routinely denied access to polling places, open demonization of their people was being publicly applauded while they stood by, frustrated, hurt, angry, and unable to overpower it. The complete disemboweling of Reconstruction via "the Mississippi Plan" of 1875 some ninety-one years previous had thoroughly accomplished its goal of the near-total disfranchisement of blacks. Simple determination to have a voice in one's government could not overcome obstacles of poll taxes and capricious constitutional-interpretation tests levied against would-be registrants. It would take more–much more.

Leaders in black communities were meeting all over the state where they could discuss these issues and potential responses unlikely to draw the notice or ire of whites. Black people jammed their churches at every available opportunity, while many whites speculated that the poor, uneducated "servant class" just liked to dress up, dance, and shout, as they were rumored to do at church. Occasionally, curious young white people would sneak over to black churches on Sunday nights and listen to soulful gospel music through open windows. Sometimes peepers told laughing stories about congregations' worship styles; sometimes they admitted liking the great music. Whatever, the services were certainly foreign spectacles to white people, most of whom had never heard the sound of applause in a sanctuary.

Because Sunday was (and still is) the most segregated day in Mississippi, many black people felt free while in church to openly discuss plans to disengage themselves from the clinging ties of their enslaved heritage. In her memoir *Barefootin'*, former Mayersville mayor Unita Blackwell, the first black woman so elected in the United States, captured the importance of church life to the black communities:

> Church was the only place we could go that was not controlled by white people, and it completed our needs in every part of our lives. The church was our anchor. It held us together. It kept us going. At a time when opportunities for entertainment were limited, the church was our main leisure-time activity. That's where we learned cooperation and leadership. Our church was a house of worship, community center, and country club. I cannot imagine my life without the church.

In 1959, church was indeed a sanctuary for many black people. Only a few years later, the unthinkable happened—bombings and burnings of African American places of worship began to scar the nightly news across the South. A line of decency was forever violated. The segregationists had figured it out.

Everyone knew it didn't take much to reach the tipping point of vicious racial outrage perpetrated by racist whites against blacks—and that outright murder wasn't an impossibility.

On the day Ella and Nelse were sitting before Justice Court Judge Rufus Watkins, Mack Charles Parker, a young black man, was arrested in Pearl River County for the alleged rape of a pregnant white woman. Later, he was transferred to the Hinds County jail for safekeeping and then transferred back to Poplarville and into a cell on the Pearl River County courthouse's third floor, following an April indictment by the county's grand jury. In the predawn hours of April 25, Parker was beaten and dragged, bleeding and fighting, from his courthouse cell by a band of hooded and masked vigilantes pounding him with clubs. Bloody handprints and drag marks of the accused left gruesome evidence of what had taken place. Ten days later, Parker's decomposing body was found floating in the Pearl River. The horrific news traveled swiftly and quietly throughout black communities of Mississippi. Despite an FBI investigation, which included setting up a field office in Poplarville, grand jury presentation, generally recognized suspects, and sheriff's cooperation, no indictments were ever made in the case, which generated sensational national headlines.

On May 14, the first public foray onto the white sand beaches of Harrison County by a group of black swimmers created a stir on the Gulf Coast. Completed in 1953 using significant taxpayer outlay, the nation's longest stretch of manmade, sugar-white beach ran alongside Highway 90 in Gulfport and Biloxi. Dr. Gilbert Mason, a black Gulfport physician, and seven other blacks, including five children, were in the midst of enjoying an afternoon at the beach when the presence of black bodies on white sand drew the attention of local law enforcement. Officers ordered the unusual sunbathers off the public property, telling them, "Negroes don't come to the sand beaches."

The incident led to eventual offers of a segregated section of beach by local officials, a declined "olive branch." A "separate but equal" sand beach was not a designation the coastal black community intended to accept.

Meanwhile, the *Gulfport Pictorial Review*, a scant weekly published by Preston W. Darling, printed an editorial stating, in part, "There is little dought [sic] that some negroes need to bathe," and "it would be very dangerous to try mixing races on this beach" due to "the difference in family and sex training between most white women and negro men." The editorial ended with a threat that if the push to integrate the beaches continued, "the people of Harrison County and the area would make the [Emmett] Till and Parker cases look like kid stuff."

The event was a preliminary skirmish in a protracted battle for the beaches that included a bloody white mob attack against black participants a year later during a "wade-in" led by Dr. Mason and an eight-year court battle, eventually resulting in a federal declaration stating that Mississippi had, in fact, engaged in racial discrimination in the matter.

In 1959, the majority of white folks in Mississippi were dead serious about keeping black people "in their places." There was, of course, the ruffian Ku Klux Klan element who terrorized the blacks, but silk-stockinged actual "Heirs of the Lost Aristocracy" saw need for something more refined with which to associate themselves. Shortly after the 1954 *Brown V Board of Education* decision portended the end of neatly segregated public schools in Mississippi and throughout the South, some Mississippi gentry created the "Citizens' Councils." They styled themselves as bastions of community leadership and orderliness. Moneyed and landed elite white males of society belonged to council chapters, which had begun in Indianola and blossomed forth quickly to all areas in the state. Unlike their Klan brethren, who employed fist and fire to subdue the "Negroes," Citizens' Council members imposed economic pressure on the unruly. Many council members were business owners, and assertive African Americans soon learned that any effort on their part to step out of their deferential roles would mean swift unemployment, not only for them, but also for their relatives. The councils proved to be very effective in their mission.

In addition to local white organizing efforts, the legislature had seen fit to fund its own state agency–the State Sovereignty Commission–to ensure that segregation remained the order of Mississippi society.

The hope of first-class citizenship juxtaposed against the hard hand of the State comprised the predominant topics of hushed discussions in both the Dorroh Hill and Lee Street communities during the summer of 1959.

Such was the backdrop against which Ella and Jewell and their supporting cast would launch a completely unscripted stage show.

A Break in the Clouds

For Ella, a day in court and possibly many nights in jail experiencing the horrors waiting inside skulked in the future. Only Nelse really knew how she was feeling because he too was struggling under the same cloud. His offense was simply "drunk driving," or maybe reckless driving–either charge was a quick misdemeanor with little punishment expected. Her offenses, on the other hand, intimidating or interfering with an officer and carrying a concealed weapon with inference that she was threatening to shoot someone in uniform, were charges fearfully recompensed by white juries.

Trying to act "normal" under the circumstances was like sloshing through knee-deep swamp water every minute of every waking hour while singing from a hymnal.

Ella didn't work as much at the nursing home after the March 27 hearing. Occasionally, she would just report in that she couldn't work that day. Jewell never asked a question, and Ella's role as head cook was preserved and honored as though she were in the kitchen as usual.

The two women tried to see each other every day anyway. Ella would sometimes go over to the McMahans' so she could see "her baby" Mike. She loved to take him apple turnovers. The child was always smiling. And Jewell would pay visits to the house on Lee Street during the day when the two women could enjoy their friendship undisturbed. They tried to talk about other things instead of the case, but it was hard.

And, there were other pressures on the Gastons.

It was not easy being a parent of a black teenager in Mississippi. Black youths who ran in public were immediately suspected of a crime. And, some white men's obsession with the black males' mythological sexual prowess was more often than not the root cause of lynchings in the South. It didn't take much to set off that powder keg. Meeting a white woman's eyes or accidentally bumping into one was an invitation to terror, too many young black men had discovered. Only four years earlier, fourteen-year-old Emmett Till had been lynched in the Delta for allegedly whistling at one.

The Gaston daughters were strong and smart. Ella made sure they knew that her brightest important hope for all of her children was that they'd get an education. An education could never be taken away from them, no matter how bad things got in Mississippi.

During the summer of 1959, while black people in Mississippi were sweltering through the Democratic Party's demeaning primary ceremonies, those in the rest of the country were beginning to break into the world of professional recognition. Ella Fitzgerald received a Grammy; William Wright became the first black to win a major golf tournament; Benjamin O. Davis Jr. became the first black general-major in the United States Air Force; and slugger Hank Aaron was unanimously voted to play in the All-Star game. These feats were told over and over in the oral tradition to make sure the achievements would be known by young and old in the African American community. There just wasn't a lot said about them in the mainstream media of Mississippi.

Just as the election year was creeping toward a frenzied August ending in the Democratic Party primaries, so too was the raft of *State v. Gaston(s)* paperwork headed toward the Noxubee County courtroom of Circuit Judge John D. Greene Jr.

On April 21, the justice of the peace court documents were filed in Noxubee County Circuit Court Cause No. 3644 *State v. Ella Gaston*. They included the February 24 affidavit of Emmett Farrar that had been read aloud in March.

The arrest warrant, issued for Ella on the same day, was filed into evidence in April.

Almost immediately, after the initial hearing before Rufus Watkins back in February, it became evident that there was a problem with the case paperwork. It wasn't completely unusual—as a rule, these cases against black people were handily dispensed with. Little attention was paid to the trifling details of dates and deadlines or even accurate charges. The documents going forward to circuit court for the Gastons had varying dates and accusations, creating a confounding tangle to be sorted through. There may have been enough to call in a motion to dismiss on "technicalities," but to try to have charges thrown over sloppy record keeping was shaky ground, which didn't stop the prosecution from trying.

On August 17, the State filed a motion to dismiss Ella's appeal from the justice of the peace judgment and requested the court to issue a writ of procedendo to Judge Woodfin, requiring him to enforce his own ruling against the defendant. Prosecutors pointed to three irregularities to support the motion:

1) The justice of the peace had failed to file a record of the March 27 court proceedings to circuit court.
2) The order from Judge Watkins transferring the case to his colleague had not been filed in circuit court.
3) The appeal bond paper showed the activity had taken place in Forrest County court, not in Noxubee County court, and was returnable to the county court of Forrest County.

"The State of Mississippi further objects and excepts to all of the above mentioned defects, deficiencies and discrepancies in the record of said appeal." So attested E. H. Britton, County Attorney; Senator W. B. Lucas; and Ernest L. Brown, special counsel for the State of Mississippi. A signature absent from the document was that of H. C. Carter, the one-term district attorney who was fighting to keep his seat.

Jesse filed a motion to amend the bond, requesting that wherever the word "Forest" [sic] appeared in the appeal bond, "Noxubee" should be inserted, explaining that the defendant resided in Forrest County, and the erroneously labeled appeal bond "was treated by all parties concerned as an appeal to the Circuit Court of Noxubee County, Mississippi."

Judge Woodfin also produced the record of proceedings of the case he'd heard on March 27 wherein Ella Gaston was "attempting to impede or hinder the arrest of her husband, Nelse Gaston." The record included Woodfin's order instructing Ella to pay a fine of twenty-five dollars and all costs of the court and serve sixty days in county jail "at hard labor," having been found guilty of the crime of "obstructing justice." Importantly, it also included the statement of Emmett Farrar declaring he had arrested Ella Gaston and taken her to jail.

There was, as of yet, no need for the Gastons and McMahans to make the dreaded trek up to Macon, but they were all prepared to do so with little warning. Jewell in particular was confident they could make it to the courtroom in ample time, no matter how short the notice.

Jesse had advised his clients to stay put in Hattiesburg while the paperwork wrangling was underway. The trial may be delayed because of it.

On August 19, following a hearing in open court, Judge Greene denied the state's motion to dismiss the defendant's appeal with a writ of procedendo, citing it as "not well taken." Further, he ordered all the paperwork concerning the bond to be amended to state "Noxubee" instead of "Forest" and "Circuit" to be substituted for "County" as to the type of court of jurisdiction. Watkins's March 25 order turning the case over to Woodfin based on the fact that Watkins's son-in-law was indirectly involved in "certain circumstances and facts which probably will be developed in the trial of said case" was also produced and made a part of the court record.

Sadly, Watkins had died unexpectedly of a massive heart attack on Independence Day. Among his pallbearers were Sheriff Farrar, Deputy Hutcherson, and Trooper Staten.

Next up, Jesse filed a Motion to Quash (set aside) the sheriff's affidavit asserting it did not sufficiently charge the offense because it did not sufficiently charge a criminal code violation. It did not charge that any threats were made by the defendant. It did not sufficiently charge that Ella had used force. Finally, it failed to charge that Ella had used any actions sufficient according to law to "either intimidate or impede the sheriff in the discharge of any lawful duty."

As insurance, Jesse also filed a Demurrer to the Affidavit, an action that didn't dispute the facts of the charges, but detailed why the defendant believed the State didn't have sufficient reason to prevail in the charges. As reason for the demurrer, Jesse essentially reiterated reasons cited in the Motion to Quash.

Aware he might be trying the Court's patience, Jesse appended affirmative post-script certifications to both documents stating the motion was "not filed for the purpose of delay, but is filed in order that justice may be done, and in my opinion the same should be sustained."

Judge Greene adjourned court that afternoon with a promise his decision on the two last filings would be rendered timely. On Friday, August 21, he overruled both the Motion to Quash and the demurrer, done, as he noted, before "the Jury to try this Cause is empanelled."

Judge Greene also signed an order continuing Cause No. 3644 until the February 1960 term of court, along with the other cases concerning the Gastons.

News of the continuance order came down from the little white office on Jefferson Street in Macon to the hulking granite structure on East Front Street in Hattiesburg. Continuance meant life for the McMahans and Gastons could proceed somewhat normally at least through Christmas.

Tuesday, August 25, was Democratic primary runoff day. Sheriff Farrar and his men were preoccupied with securing his continuation as the major law enforcement officer for Noxubee County. Marian was battling it out against A. J. Hammack, despite assurances and reassurances that her election as sheriff would guarantee things would remain the same. She had dispensed with two other challengers in the August 4 primary.

District Attorney Carter eventually lost to the young challenger, Buck, 1,373 to 841 in the runoff; Allen Lanier failed to realize his dream of becoming a gun-toting, siren-blasting constable, losing to incumbent Jernigan 451 to 308 in a three-man field. Marian Farrar successfully succeeded her husband as sheriff, defeating Hammack 1,292 to 933.

Idle Time

Well, Stennis had bought them a bit of breathing room, Jewell reasoned, though it didn't make waiting on the new court date any easier than waiting on the last one had been. She was completely determined that Ella would never go back to jail. Ella had never told her a thing about what had happened to her the night she stayed at the Noxubee County jail, which was reported to look less like a jail than any structure possibly could. Jewell knew it had been bad, though, because Ella Gaston had come out forever changed.

Where she had formerly been outgoing and jubilant, Ella was now introspective and more serious. There would be long stretches when Ella would sit quietly and simply look–straight ahead, in the sky, or at her folded hands. The experience had been clearly devastating, whatever it was. And, as the first court date had drawn closer and closer, Ella had seemed to retreat even further into herself. She was visibly relieved when the case was continued, but, soon enough, the light in her eyes would begin to wander off again.

During some of their afternoon visits at Ella's, the two women took on the serious topic of what they'd do if it came right down to keeping Ella out of jail. If she were convicted, as Jesse promised she would be, they both figured there likely would be a lapse between whatever might happen at the Supreme Court and Ella's actually being put in a cell. The dilemma was how to keep the "Noxubee thugs," as Jewell liked to call them, from getting their hands on Ella. They both admitted that it wasn't an unusual thing for black people just to disappear, as they had witnessed with Frank Ed Hill, but Ella would never leave her children like that. What would really keep those white men away from her?

Yes, the likelihood was that Ella would be found guilty again in Noxubee's circuit court. Elections were over. Farrar had won in his wife's name. Incoming governor Ross Barnett was romping up and down the state and on television at every opportunity espousing the "Southern Way of Life" and railing about the "Negroes."

It would be most unusual for a jury of white men–the only people routinely allowed to serve on juries in Mississippi–to do anything but convict Ella Gaston.

Every time Jesse tried to explain to his clients the futility of hoping against a conviction, he was met by a stern "Ella will never go to jail again" from Mrs. McMahan. She was stubborn as hell on the subject, he thought. But, that didn't keep Jesse from trying to prepare them all for the inevitable–Ella would be found guilty, Jesse would appeal to the state's Supreme Court, and, if all prayers were answered, they would reverse the decision.

It was the strategy he set out on February 23, 1959, the day he got the case. He had hired the seasoned court reporter to take down testimony in the justice of the peace hearing because he felt it would be crucial to setting up the appeal. Jesse told his clients he was certain some witnesses for the prosecution would mess up their stories from one courtroom to the next. He knew this because some of them had been witnesses for him back when he himself was the prosecution.

Jesse originally thought that fighting this case against a thirty-eight-year-old, green district attorney with no prosecutorial experience would really increase Ella's odds of a win at the local level, small though they would remain. But, when W. F. Lucas's signature appeared on the writ of procedendo to return the case back to Judge Woodfin, Jesse knew the effort would be no day in the park. Harvey Buck had handed his torch to a lion in the courtroom. As a self-proclaimed tiger, Jesse prepared for a fight.

Judge Greene's generational peer, Lucas had been representing Noxubee County from the Sixteenth District in the state senate since 1944. Born in Brooksville, his profile in the state's *Official and Statistical Register* described him as a lawyer, farmer, Methodist, and member of Ole Miss's Kappa Alpha Order. A World War I veteran and thirty-third-degree Mason, Lucas was a proud member of the Sons of the Confederacy. Of course, he was a Democrat. Like many prominent men of the day, Lucas was also a member of the international fraternal organization Knights of Pythias, a group pledged to the promotion of understanding among men of good will as the surest means of attaining "Universal Peace."

Secretary of the local Citizens' Council, Lucas was also a member of the executive committee of the Mississippi Association of Citizens' Councils, representing Macon.

Lucas had been part of a legislative contingent that wanted to pull funding from the Sovereignty Commission, the state's agency charged with maintaining Mississippi's Jim Crow laws and intensely segregated society. Their idea was to funnel money to the local Citizens' Councils who appeared to be doing a better job of maintaining order in their own communities than the commission appeared to be doing in the state.

The election of Ross Barnett made the legislative funding fight moot. Almost immediately after his administration began, the Sovereignty Commission donated twenty thousand dollars to the state councils' association. It was the first in a series of donations, the rest in five thousand dollar increments, totaling at least two hundred thousand dollars over time. So, in addition to funding a public agency to maintain segregation, Mississippi taxpayers also underwrote social clubs devoted to doing the same thing.

Bryce and Bill made another trip to Macon to see Counselor Stennis after the holidays. When they left, the two men understood clearly the threat they were facing. It wasn't just an unpopular stand they were taking by helping their black employees; it was downright dangerous. Jesse warned them that racial tensions, recently exacerbated by the highly charged election cycle rhetoric, were at an all-time high, more than he'd seen during his own lifetime. The least little thing could incite a bloody battle, he cautioned.

"We all must be careful–very careful," he said. The men agreed and carried the message home to Hattiesburg.

Jewell reminded everyone that she carried a gun, and she knew how to use it.

THE TRIAL

On Parade

Trial day was Thursday, February 17, 1960, the day before Ella's forty-seventh birthday. The troupe from Hattiesburg realized that Jesse Stennis knew what he was talking about when they caught their first glimpse of the sparkling Noxubee County Courthouse. Its lawn was packed with men, mostly white. They were congregated in groups, some leaning on the Confederate statue's base. A couple were draped across the cannon beneath it. A few were sitting on broad limestone steps underlining the building's expansive front portico, braced with six white Tuscan columns in the Jeffersonian style and topped with a pediment bearing a large black and white clock face. Some just stood around in the yard smoking and spitting.

Two Confederate flags flapped from the flagpole as accompaniment to the statue and cannon. The one on top was the official flag of the Confederacy, the "Blood-Stained Banner," and the other was the more familiar Beauregard battle flag of crossed blue bars with white stars on a field of red. The flags' identities would be explained in the *Macon Beacon* later in the year by Sheriff Marian Farrar in response to public inquiries. She wanted to make sure everyone knew the distinction between the Confederacy's "official" flag and the ubiquitous battle flag. The brightly colored symbols left no doubt as to where Noxubee County decision-makers' hearts and minds lay. After all, the national commander of the Sons of Confederate Veterans in 1958 had been proud native son Postmaster T. W. Crigler of Macon. There was nary a Mississippi nor United States flag to be seen.

It was eight o'clock in the morning, according to the courthouse clock, as the black Lincoln with a Forrest County tag slowly made its way down Jefferson Street. Its occupants—Bryce and Jewell in front, and Ella and Nelse in back—were silent for a minute.

"Where's the parade?" Jewell quipped when she saw the crowd.

"I think we're it," Nelse said, and they all chuckled nervously.

Bill and another supporter from Hattiesburg were in the car behind them.

Stennis had rightly feared they'd have to walk a gauntlet to get to the building's front doors, so he'd advised Bryce and Bill to park in the back and come through the back door entrance. Nelse and Ella were expected to go down the back steps and enter through the basement, as befitting their underling status, but not on this day. No sir.

All talk stopped as the foursome made their way across the parking lot and up the back stairs. Across the back of the building, tall paned windows framed white faces. Black custodial workers stepped aside as the Hattiesburg folks passed by.

Walking side by side, the four made quite a striking ensemble for the expectant onlookers.

Defendant Mrs. Gaston wore a modest, store-bought tan suit, pearls, clear stockings, and low-heeled pumps. Jewell and Ella had conferred on Ella's wardrobe for the occasion, making sure she looked just right. "Understated refinement" was the image they wanted to achieve. Ella carried a good-looking handbag and wore makeup and lipstick—but not too much.

Mr. Gaston was dressed in a dark jacket over dress slacks, a crisp white shirt, plain tie, and flawless Stacy Adams shoes. He strolled toward the courthouse in the slow and deliberate way a strong, handsome man walks when he knows all eyes are on him.

Jewell thought, as usual, that Nelse was a good-looking man. Though the McMahans had no idea that a white shirt on a black man was tantamount to a bull's-eye in Noxubee County, Nelse certainly knew it. He proceeded into the courthouse straight-backed and firm.

The black onlookers nodded approvingly.

Both Jewell and Bryce turned out in conventional business suits. They too made a striking pair: she with rhinestone-studded cat-eye glasses, exceptionally high heels, and a handbag big enough to carry a gun; he, broad, tall, and resolute—obviously someone who was taken very, very seriously.

Inside, their greetings went unreturned as the group sought out the familiar face of Jesse Stennis.

The red-brick courthouse was the pride of Noxubee County. It had opened in 1952 on the site of the previous courthouse that had burned. Inside were polished terrazzo granite floors, marble and granite wainscoting, county offices with dark oak frames and doors, and a pair of dramatic marble staircases leading to an open lobby on the second floor centered with a ten-foot-tall double-hung window, large enough to accommodate someone stepping out onto an ornate cast-iron balcony overlooking the front lawn. The beautifully sunlit courtroom upstairs, with tidy "marble" linoleum squares on its floor, was arranged with pew seating and a traditional bar and bench. Jurors sat in colonial style swivel chairs, and counselors' tables were nearly adjacent to each other, facing the elevated judge's seat. Witnesses testified from the raised witness box between the lawyers and the jury, facing the audience. The attorneys' podium, where

Bull Deale's head had rested a few years before, remained in place, facing the bench.

Jesse was waiting for them in the second-floor lobby along with Bill. The lawyer warned them again that this case had turned into something very important as evidenced by the large crowd of onlookers. Once inside, Ella took her seat at the defense table beside Jesse, and her husband and the other companions sat behind her on one of the cherry pews reserved for onlookers, the bar with its delicate, spindle posts separating them. The room filled rapidly with both blacks and whites. Blacks sat together in the back; Ella and Nelse nodded at some of them who were their family members. While nearly all in the audience appeared to be very rural with few financial resources, Jewell noted that several white men of apparent means had also joined the onlookers. She recognized a couple of them from the first justice of the peace hearing a year before.

Seated prominently in the front and facing the audience was Emmett Farrar, now Chief Deputy Farrar.

Soon, the prosecutors' table began to fill up. Senator Lucas took his place as lead, and County Attorney E. H. Britton and Lucas's law partner, Ernest L. Brown, joined him. District Attorney Buck was absent. He was down the hall in the company of his first Grand Jury.

The senator reached out his hand across the two-foot distance dividing the tables.

"Mr. Stennis," he said.

"Senator," Jesse replied as he shook the older man's hand. Like Jesse, the senator had once served as district attorney of the Sixteenth District, as had Jesse's second cousin John C. Stennis before him.

"All rise! Oyez! Oyez! Oyez! The court of the Honorable John D. Greene Jr., Judge of the Sixteenth Circuit Court District of the State of Mississippi, is now in session. God save the State of Mississippi and this Honorable Court," intoned the chief deputy as spectators rustled to their feet and the stately Judge Greene swept into his courtroom.

"You may be seated," the judge allowed as he arranged himself at the bench. It was nine o'clock.

At sixty-eight, Judge Greene was a large man with a booming voice and a demeanor that usually meant all business for those who stood before his bench. He had been a public servant for a very long time. As a youth, Greene had worked on the family farm at Sturgis and was self-educated, though he taught in the public schools of Oktibbeha County for two years while he read law. He attended the University of Mississippi for a while and was awarded his law degree in June 1915, the same year he was elected to the State House of Representatives. He chaired the Registration and Election Committee his freshman term.

Greene had gained his judicial seat by appointment of Governor Fielding Wright when his predecessor, John C. Stennis, won the unexpired term of deceased United States Senator Bilbo in 1947. In 1958, Judge Greene had been challenged after his second full term by Jesse Stennis, who stood before him today. The two were professionally polite to each other, as lawyers are trained to be.

For the Gaston case, a number of local white men had been pulled in the regular venire to select jurors. Jewell noted their appearance. The daughter of Judge Blaine Clark was well aware of what dress and decorum were supposed to look like inside a courtroom. She found the potential jurors' shabby appearance to be surprising and pitiful.

Jewell actually felt kind of sorry for them. As a collection, they looked like wretched old things—not one of them had dressed up, and when they spoke, they used poor language, she noted.

Before voir dire of the jury began, Jesse requested preliminary proceedings to be made a part of the court record. The judge granted the unusual request, court reporter Bessie Kate Bell pulled out her stenography pad, and jury selection commenced.

During the initial filtering of juror candidates through the sieve of personal, familial, and professional relationships, Jesse objected to perceived badgering of one individual by the senator, alleging the man was being held up to public ridicule over his nephew's recent conviction. Judge Greene overruled, the first of many such decisions to come.

Lucas appropriated the jury selection process to lay out the prosecution's case, in so many words:

> Now, gentlemen of the jury, applicable to all, this is a case in which the defendant sitting over here, a negro woman living in Hattiesburg, is under trial here at this time charged with the intimidation of an officer. Now that means that when Mr. Farrar undertook to talk to her and her husband, probably place them one or both under arrest, that the manner in which she undertook to intimidate him was to reach in her pocket book and get a .30-caliber, automatic pearl handled, nickel plated pistol, which will be produced here, the State will produce it, in a manner that led everyone to believe that she was going to shoot it. The state will prove that she made the statement that you are not going to arrest my husband for nothing and at the time she made the statement her husband was being talked to by the sheriff on a matter of being drunk and driving while drunk and in that state of affairs, after telling him that you are not going to arrest my husband for nothing, she reached in the pocketbook, the sheriff

grabbed her hand and when he held her hand back
in there and made her drop what she had in her
hand, it turned out to be an automatic pistol, so
the State contends that she in this intimidation was
attempting to shoot the sheriff.

The two lawyers engaged in back-and-forth tussles over who was
kin to whom among the jury pool and the passel of attorneys. When
it was his turn to address the panel, Jesse cautioned jurors against
believing the senator's assertions about charges against Ella.

Gentlemen, I would like to see this question of all
of you, and I would like a specific answer from you,
This woman here is charged with, as Mr. Lucas says,
intimidating the sheriff, Mr. Emmett Farrar, by
reaching in her pocketbook and getting a pistol in
such a manner that everyone around there thought
that she was going to use the pistol on the sheriff.
Now that is Mr. Lucas' statement of the facts. I ask
you if you will rely solely on what the testimony
develops here instead of what one of the lawyers in
the case might say is the fact? If you will I would like
to see your hand, gentlemen? If you will rely solely
on the testimony that comes from the witness stand
rather than on the statement of any of the lawyers
in the case, if you will rely on the testimony, the
sworn testimony, that comes to you, I would like to
see your hand, gentlemen?

After a further gleaning of the jury pool, Stennis again questioned
the candidates' resolve to be fair.

Gentlemen, one other question. Is there any reason why if you are placed in this jury, charged with the responsibility of passing on the guilt or innocence of this defendant, is there any reason that you can't give this defendant a fair trial? If there is I would like to see your hand, whether you have been asked about it or not? In your heart you know whether there is or not? Now Mr. Lucas I believe made you a proposition on discharging this defendant and I would like to ask you this. If the State fails to prove, beyond a reasonable doubt, by competent evidence that this defendant did reach in her pocketbook and get a pistol to shoot the sheriff with and the sheriff made her drop it, if the State fails to prove that by competent evidence, beyond a reasonable doubt, will you find the defendant not guilty?

The senator interjected, "Wait just a second. Now we object to that, if Your Honor please, because that proposition was not put to the jury in the manner and form as stated by counsel."

"Well, the jury heard the statements and the objection will be overruled. This is just a preliminary skirmish here," Judge Greene decided.

There were some final questions about whether or not any jurors had heard the case discussed within the community, which they all denied, and counsel left the courtroom to pass on the jury. Judge Greene took the opportunity to retreat to his chambers, and the women from Hattiesburg headed for the nearest restroom.

There was a problem. When Jewell asked a woman in the downstairs circuit clerk's office where Ella and she could find the ladies' room, she learned there were no accommodations for black people inside the courthouse. Ella would have to go outside and down the back stairs into the "colored" restrooms in the back basement.

"Humpf," Jewell said.

Shortly afterward, Ella and Jewell were side by side in use of the nicely appointed "Whites Only" women's facilities, also in the basement, but accessible from the first-floor lobby and equipped with private granite stalls. Bryce was standing in the stairwell just above the restroom door with his massive arms crossed over his broad chest.

Everyone regained their places, stood up, sat down, and Judge Greene announced the jury.

> I am going to call out the names of the twelve men who will try this case and you will remain in the box. I will start out on jury No. 1. Now follow me, gentlemen. Mine [the venire list] is marked all over too. The first one on there is Mr. George Finch, Mr. Clark, Mr. Upchurch, Mr. Davis, that is J. W. Davis, and James H. Butler and George D. Conner, that is on No. 1, and on No. 2 there is Fred A. Ogletree and Rhoden Butler and then H. L. Davis and Elisha Clark and Lloyd L. Conner, and down on three there is Mr. Thomas E. Butler on three. Now the rest of you gentlemen may stand aside and you twelve men get up there in the box and let's see if we have got twelve before you leave.

The judge and lawyers all counted heads.

Judge Greene pronounced, "By agreement of the attorneys, you gentlemen won't have to stay together. Go on out and eat your lunch and come back as quick as you can." He followed with the usual admonishment not to talk about the case. Court would resume at 1:00 p.m.

Bryce told Jewell that he and Bill would stay in the courthouse and confer with Jesse if she wanted to take Nelse and Ella to get something to eat.

So off they went, this time out the front door—not that it was more convenient; it was just more important. Jewell and the Gastons walked around behind the building, got into the car with Ella riding shotgun, and headed across Jefferson Street to the first eating establishment they saw.

Jewell went in ahead of the others. "We want to get lunch," she told the woman at the counter.

"Can't serve you," the woman said, never meeting her eye.

"Why not?"

"You got those niggers with you."

So Jewell and the Gastons set off on foot down the street to another lunch spot where they were met with similar resistance.

"Are you being threatened?" Jewell asked the embarrassed bearer of the rejection.

The waitress nodded and looked the other way.

The trio trotted back to the car and headed for a nearby service station, expecting to purchase snacks.

"We need to get some lunch," Jewell told the uniformed proprietor.

"Sorry. Can't do it," he said, wiping his hands on a greasy rag.

Jewell trudged back to her car.

"Ma'am?" a tentative voice said from behind her. She turned to see an anxious young mechanic.

"Yes?"

"Ma'am, there's a Pure Oil station outside of town where they'll serve you and the others," the nervous workman offered.

Jewell got directions, and the threesome headed out of town with high hopes, ignoring the sidewalk gawkers they were passing. Jewell and Ella were riding up front, and Nelse was in the backseat.

Once at the friendly service station, the out-of-towners were all in need of the facilities.

"Nope," said the owner when Jewell asked if they could use the toilets.

"We'll just have to go pee in the bushes, then. Ella, you take that bush; I'll take this bush; and, Nelse, you go behind the tree," Jewell instructed.

The three then ate their sandwiches in the car, had a Coke apiece, filled the tank, and headed back into town, arriving into the courtroom just before court was gaveled back into session.

Eyewitnesses

The trial began in earnest.

Witnesses were called and sworn in, and then Jesse made a second unusual request.

"We would like to have this taken by the court reporter, please, sir," he said.

"The opening of the case?" Judge Greene queried.

"Yes, sir, his opening statements."

"I never heard of that before, but I am going to let her take it if you want it. All right."

Miss Bell assumed her pose with pen and stenographer's pad.

Senator Lucas began, "On the twenty-first day of February of last year, a peace officer at Shuqualak had been molested by a darkey. The next day –"

Jesse was on his feet. "Your Honor please, we object to that statement."

"Overruled."

The senator resumed, "And the next day, Mr. Farrar, the sheriff of the county, and Mr. Hutcherson, the deputy sheriff of the county, with Mr. Allan Lanier, who had been deputized by Mr. Farrar, went out into the southwestern part of Noxubee County checking into whereabouts of one who had been charged with the felonious attack on the peace officer at Shuqualak. While out there they came in contact with the defendant over here, whose name is Ella Gaston, and her husband, perhaps some other darkies. Mr. Farrar and Mr. Hutcherson and Mr. Lanier searching for the one who had made this attack on Mr. Moore, observed the careless, reckless, driving of an automobile by the Gaston woman's husband, who he had been told was related to the party that he was searching for."

On his feet again, Jesse protested, "We are going to object to counsel's statement on that, if Your Honor please, as being prejudicial on what had been told the sheriff."

Lucas countered, "You never saw a person in your life that is freer than I am."

"Your Honor, I would like to get my objection in here without–"

"Just a minute now. Go on and make your objection," the judge ordered.

"As being highly prejudicial and hearsay, incompetent evidence about what the sheriff may or may not have been told. That is not the way to try a lawsuit, Your Honor," Jesse concluded.

Judge Greene responded by instructing the senator to merely read the affidavit.

Jesse interjected that he'd like a ruling on his objection. It was sustained, and, after Jesse insisted, jurors were instructed to disregard the remarks.

Lucas then read the affidavit word for word and took his seat.

It was Jesse's turn. Rising while buttoning his suit jacket, Jesse removed his glasses and placed them strategically in his right hand to use as a pointer. He began pacing, his voice modulating from quiet and chummy to sermonesque. He was captivating on stage, most in the courtroom were already aware. Today, the dramatic and demonstrative litigator did not disappoint.

"May it please the Court and you gentlemen of the jury, I am coming down with the flu and I may have a little trouble in making you hear me, but I will do my best. In behalf of the defendant in this case, gentlemen, the defense simply says that she is not guilty of the crime with which she is charged. Now I am going to be perfectly frank with you gentlemen. It is my duty to be and there will be no denial that she did have a pistol in her purse, and if you want to find her guilty of carrying a pistol, that is one thing, but she denies specifically, gentlemen, that she made any threats toward the sheriff, that she made any attempt to impede him in arresting Nelse Gaston, that she made no effort whatsoever to use the pistol on the sheriff or on anyone else. The defense will submit proof, which I believe will be uncontradicted, gentlemen, that this defendant here was surrounded by some four or six officers, who were all armed at the time that the pistol was taken, that her purse was taken from her, and the pistol taken out of it. As I said in the opening statement to you gentlemen here this morning, the proof will show that she did have a pistol, but that is one charge and this thing of trying to use it on an officer to try to intimidate this officer or trying to prevent him from arresting Nelse Gaston, we will present proof, gentlemen, to the fact that that just didn't happen. Thank you."

Stennis was a commanding presence in the courtroom, there was no doubt. Juxtapose him against the fiery and folksy Lucas, and the spectators would certainly get the fireworks they were hoping for. The judge maintained his usual all-business persona.

Whether or not "the rule" was invoked to keep Deputy Sheriff Farrar out of the courtroom became the next subject of debate. Invoking the rule ensured that all potential witnesses would not be inside the courtroom during testimony so as not to give anyone ideas about their own statements. Judge Greene ruled that Farrar, the state's star witness, would remain. He was also sworn to uphold peace and safety in the courtroom, and in this packed house, a rickety could erupt at any minute.

The State called Deputy Farrar as its first witness. He began to describe the Shuqualak confrontation, how Ella had come around the car to protest her husband's arrest, and then he said, "She raised a large handbag up and opened the bag and started in there with her right hand and told me I couldn't arrest him, he hadn't done anything."

Farrar then stated he'd grabbed the purse out of her hand, reached into the bag, and discovered the pistol, whereupon he had placed Ella under arrest for interfering with an officer.

Jesse made a large, sweeping note on his yellow legal pad.

Lucas next produced the pistol in question, and much was made about whether or not it had been, or was currently, loaded. The gun became Exhibit A.

Farrar explained that the stop's initial cause was for reckless driving and then, after a close observation of Nelse, Farrar placed Nelse under arrest for drunken driving. Jesse objected to Farrar's testimony regarding whether or not Nelse was arrested for "drunken driving." Overruled.

Lucas asked the deputy sheriff where he first encountered Nelse on the day in question.

"Well, I saw him somewhere that morning. I don't remember where, but we were investigating and trying to find a Negro by the name of Frank Ed Hill that had committed an assault upon the Marshal down there."

Jesse stood. "We are going to object to that, Your Honor, please, as being immaterial and irrelevant and inflammatory."

"Well, overruled. He is telling why he was down there."

Farrar went on to testify that he'd seen Nelse and Ella loading "several children" in the car in the Dorroh Hill community southwest of Shuqualak, "and that was when he left there in such a reckless manner, spinning the wheels, throwing rocks all over us and so fast I called the highway patrol to stop him for reckless driving."

For those who had ridden up and down gravelly Dorroh Hill Road, it was common knowledge that it was very hard to drive there above a crawl. For those who knew about Nelse and his loving attention to his vehicles, this part of the tale was outrageous. Jesse had warned them all not to show too much emotion during the trial. This would be a long afternoon.

Farrar elaborated on how Nelse was going so fast on Dorroh Hill Road into Shuqualak that he couldn't catch him. But the highway patrol did stop him as requested, in front of Mr. Pete Flora's house, Farrar finished.

On cross-examination, Jesse asked the former sheriff to explain his testimony about having seen Nelse earlier in the Dorroh Hill vicinity on the day of the arrest.

"I don't recall the time. I am pretty forgetful," Farrar testified.

The man had declared he was "pretty forgetful" in the middle of sworn testimony, Jewell observed.

"I remember seeing him somewhere, and that morning Mr. Rufus Watkins, who is now deceased, was with us and he knew Nelse evidently, and he asked him a few questions out there in reference to this Frank Ed Hill, as I recall it. We were interested in finding out his whereabouts," Farrar said.

Jesse asked Farrar what time the arrest happened.

"I can't say. I want to tell the thing just right. I wish I could remember the exact time, but I don't recall the time. It wasn't in the late afternoon though. It was sometime along I would think around two thirty or three o'clock."

He had called ahead to the highway patrol to stop the Ford Fairlane, Farrar testified, and said that by the time he arrived on the scene, Nelse was behind the car and Patrolman Richardson was with him.

Jesse wanted to know if Nelse was looking for his driver's license.

"I don't know. He may have been. I am not saying he wasn't, but when I got out, I walked up there and I says, 'Nigger, you are under arrest for reckless driving.' That is the first word I said to him."

Jesse designed the next exchange to confound the witness and solidify his inconsistent testimony from justice court to circuit court.

"Did Ella get out of the car and come around the car before or after someone had hit Nelse, her husband?"

"She got out of the car and come around and stood in front of Nelse before anyone hit him. I didn't see anyone hit Nelse. I heard a lick."

"You heard a lick?"

"Yes, sir. She told me that I couldn't arrest him before I heard the lick."

"I see. Who was it struck him, Mr. Sheriff?" Jesse asked.

"Mr. Hutcherson was standing there by me helping me and–"

"She was, where was Ella when Mr. Hutcherson hit Nelse?"

"Facing me."

"Facing you?"

"And Nelse was behind her and Hutcherson over to the side there," Farrar explained.

"She had gotten out of the car and was facing you when Mr. Hutcherson hit Nelse? Is that right?"

"Yes, sir, that is what I said, and she had also just spoke to me before Hutcherson hit Nelse."

Farrar didn't even recognize what had just happened to him.

An interlude discussion ensued concerning Ella's handbag and whether she had put her hand in it, when Jesse sharpened his knife for the plunge.

"Mr. Farrar, I believe you testified in the justice of the peace court in this case, did you not?

"Yes, sir."

"At that time I asked you, 'Who was it that hit Nelse Gaston?' and you said that 'Didn't anybody hit him.'

"I told you I didn't know, to ask Hutcherson if anyone hit him and he would tell you if he hit him or not, and I told you I heard a lick in justice court, but I didn't see it. I was looking at Ella," Farrar defended himself.

The deputy sheriff left the witness stand, adjusting his gun belt as he went.

The Setup

District Attorney Buck handled the direct examination of Deputy O'Dell (Bill) Hutcherson, the man who had subdued Alec Bailey in that very courtroom two years prior.

Hutcherson, too, explained the lawmen's motive for being in Shuqualak that day.

"Well, we had gone down there, the sheriff and myself and Allen Lanier, looking for a Negro that had jumped on the marshal the night before."

Jesse jerked off his glasses and leaped up to object. He implored the court to direct the jury to disregard the testimony. Overruled.

Hutcherson was asked to describe his version of what happened.

"Well, we were out near Dorroh Hill out there, a place they call Dorroh Hill. There was Nelse Gaston and Ella and several children and several other Negroes standing around the car out there, and we had stopped. We had some information that we might locate this party we were looking for out there. They were loading up in the car and then Nelse took off in the car and loaded up the children."

Buck asked for a departure description.

Hutcherson explained that the officers were standing outside the sheriff's pickup on Dorroh Hill Road when Nelse took off, slinging rocks all over them.

"Well, after he loaded them in the car, why, he took off at such a high rate of speed the car was just wobbling all over the road and throwing gravel and rocks everywhere ... so we got in the pickup. We seen we couldn't catch them so we called the highway patrol and asked them to stop him."

Asked what he was doing while the sheriff was busy arresting Ella and looking into her handbag, Hutcherson said, "Well, Nelse was standing there leaning up against the back of the car fumbling through his billfold looking for his driver's license, and when Ella come around and told the sheriff he couldn't arrest her husband because he hadn't did nothing, why, the sheriff turned to her and I told Nelse, I said, 'You are under arrest. Put your hands up.' Well, he laughed at me and paid me no attention, and I hit him."

"Did he put his hands up when you told him?"

"No, sir, and I hit him, and he put his hands up," Hutcherson testified.

Buck wanted to know what had been done with the defendants after their arrests.

"Well, we put them in the car and brought Nelse on up here to the jail, and they had all those children, a carload of them, and the sheriff told Ella that he would just let her go back out there with her people and keep those children that night and come on up here the next morning because he didn't want to bring all them children up here, didn't have no place to put them."

Ella's back got straighter, as did Jewell's.

"He locked Nelse up?"

"Yes, sir."

"But he did not lock the defendant, Ella, up?"

"He let her go out there and stay with some of her people and stay with those children because there was no one to stay with them."

Ella looked down at her hands, folded primly in her lap. Jewell readjusted her crossed legs.

Buck and Hutcherson discussed the pistol in evidence, whether or not it was loaded then and now, where it had been stored, and whether it was the same one found in Ella's handbag.

Jesse was ready on cross. He drew a plain picture between Hutcherson's testimony in this court as opposed to what he'd said during the justice court hearing. Eventually, and in his own words, Hutcherson contradicted his previous testimony about whether or not the gun had been loaded when it was confiscated, whether or not he had actually seen the gun in the purse, whether or not the sheriff had arrested Nelse for reckless driving or driving while intoxicated on the scene or later, en route to the jail—all pieces that would help reasonable persons decide whether or not Ella had, in fact, interfered with her husband's arrest or intimidated the arresting officer, whichever charge would eventually prevail.

Hutcherson revealed that highway patrol officer Charlie Staten had actually been inside Pete Flora's house when Farrar and his deputies, all riding in the front seat of a pickup, arrived on the scene. Hutcherson appeared confused about whether he had actually seen or had previously testified to Ella's opening her bag, placing her hand inside it just so, as the sheriff had claimed earlier on the stand, and whether or not the sheriff pulled the gun from the handbag. Hutcherson finally concluded that he first saw the pistol when the sheriff pulled it out of Ella's handbag. Whether the purse had a snap or handles, though, he couldn't recall.

If testimony could have been any more tedious, Jewell couldn't imagine it, but she recognized Jesse's drive to show inconsistencies in the officers' testimonies to prepare for what they all knew was coming–an appeal to the Mississippi Supreme Court. Whether the jury was following the trail Jesse left prominently on display, no one could tell. At least one man in the jury box was asleep.

Buck opted for redirect and got around to asking whether there were any other firearms in the vehicle.

"Yes, sir, there was a .22 rifle under the seat of the car."

Jesse was on his feet once again, hand and glasses pointing in the air. "We are going to object to that, if Your Honor please. It is immaterial and irrelevant and inflammatory."

The judge's response was stunning. It wasn't an outright ruling; no, it was something else altogether.

"Well, the Court has been very liberal in letting in a lot of incompetent proof here. I am going to let that in, in my opinion. When we are talking about this other party, I think too much of that has gone in already. Go ahead and answer the question. You found a rifle, whether you did or not."

Seldom had the counselors heard a judge admit his own mistakes from the bench–or anywhere else, for that matter–not to mention allowing such a statement into the court record.

"Yes, sir, a .22 rifle."

The court's solicitous response: "All right, come on down. You come down, Bill."

The State, again represented by Senator Lucas, called its next witness, former highway patrolman R. L. Richardson, who testified that he had been sitting in the patrol car in Pete Flora's front yard when a call came in from Farrar describing Nelse's car and asking for assistance in getting him stopped. "He said he was behind a '58 Ford that he didn't look like he was going to get them stopped and see if I could stop them. They were coming off the Dorroh Hill Road."

Richardson described who was in the car. "This Negro man, Gaston, and the defendant and I couldn't recall, five or six or seven small Negro kids."

"I see," Lucas said.

"All sizes," the witness finished.

Next, Richardson described his version of how the sheriff had come upon Ella's pistol, which he testified started as a tussle over her purse.

On cross, Jesse honed in on whether or not Richardson had previously testified that he saw Ella pull her purse up and away from the sheriff when he asked what was in it. Jesse wanted jurors to know that Richardson had told Justice of the Peace Woodfin that Ella's reaction had been the opposite of trying to get her hand into her purse.

The former highway patrolman couldn't remember what he'd testified to, even when his testimony was read back to him, very slowly and with extreme enunciation, by Jesse. Richardson did, however, make it clear that he didn't see Ella pull a pistol on the sheriff, nor did he see her put her hands in the purse—both essential components of the state's intimidation charge against Jesse's client.

"Now, Mr. Richardson, you of course realize that you are under your oath and you are a former officer of the State highway patrol? I want to ask you to tell this jury whether or not on that occasion, after Nelse Gaston was arrested, Ella Gaston made any attempt to threaten you or any other officers down there?"

"Repeat that question, Mr. Stennis, I don't believe I got it."

Stennis repeated himself as slowly and methodically as possible. "Did you hear her threaten anybody down there in your presence on that occasion?"

"No, sir."

Richardson had denied that Ella threatened an officer, one of the key allegations against her.

Senator Lucas handled direct questioning of the next witness, Special Deputy Allen Lanier, who testified that he had been present when the sheriff questioned Nelse out on Dorroh Hill about where he was going. Nelse had said Hattiesburg. Allen said he, Hutcherson, and Farrar were the officers present.

"Now, who was with Gaston at that time?"

"It was his wife and about six or eight Negro children."

Lanier testified that Nelse "looked kind of funny but he was hanging on, standing by the side of the car." He said Nelse appeared to be under the influence of liquor. Jesse objected; the court overruled.

"Allen, what did Gaston do when he left there? How did he leave?" Lucas asked.

"Well, he just slammed the door and stepped in the car and raced the motor and took off."

"I see. What did the sheriff do?" Lucas continued.

"The sheriff said, 'Let's go get him,' says, 'Anybody that got no more respect for us than that, us right here and throwing gravel back on us, let's go.'"

Lanier's testimony was full of repeated conversations, and Jesse's objections for hearsay were continually overruled.

Judge Greene finally admitted, "I think we are getting too much in there anyway about this other case, this husband, all this catching him and all that, but go ahead and get down to the meat in the coconut."

"All right, here comes the meat. Did you see Gaston after he left Dorroh Hill?" the senator asked.

"Yes, sir."

After establishing that Lanier next saw Nelse behind his car with a highway patrolman, Lucas asked the special deputy whether Nelse appeared drunk or sober at the time.

Exasperated, Jesse continued to object to descriptions of Nelse being drunk. Finally, Judge Greene agreed that Lanier was not a qualified police officer who could testify as a professional about someone's apparent drunkenness.

Lanier's testimony about Ella's arrest was a close reflection of that which had gone previously, including in which hand Ella had clutched her purse and what she'd said.

"Well, she came from around the car and she walked up, walking up in the, between her, the sheriff and Hutcherson and Richardson and myself were standing and she came walking up there and she came up with her purse with the left hand and started in it with the right."

On cross, Jesse tried to show Lanier had previously known Nelse and his daddy, but Judge Greene stopped the line of questioning. Trying to elicit confirmation from Lanier that he had heard Nelse say he and his family were headed back to Hattiesburg drew another admonishment from the bench.

"Well, that is repetition three or four times. Let's go along," Judge Greene directed.

Jesse turned his attention to the purse.

"Did you see Ella Gaston unsnap the purse?"

"No, sir." Lanier explained that he thought it had already been open. He repeated that she was reaching into it with her right hand.

Jesse took some time to get Lanier to agree that there were at least five fully armed officers within close range of the defendant.

Surely it was obvious to the jury that it would have been pretty remarkable for someone like the prim, dainty defendant, Ella Gaston, to pull a gun on anybody under those circumstances. Surely.

Lanier continued to assert that he had not heard the sheriff ask Ella what she had in her purse.

The state called Marshal Ollice Moore.

Jesse stood up again.

"I object to Mr. Moore because he has been in the courtroom. For the record, I would like to state this. At the beginning of this proceeding, Your Honor announced that the rule would be invoked, and the witness Otis Moore was in the courtroom during the trial," Jesse said.

Judge Greene addressed Lucas: "It was agreed by the state that he would not be called."

Lucas promised, "We will not call him now or any other time, never as long as we live."

The state next called Circuit Clerk J. E. McDavid to certify venue as being in Noxubee County, State of Mississippi, District Four, Shuqualak, and that R. R. Watkins Sr. had original jurisdiction over the case.

Jesse had reserved the right to recall all State's witnesses. He asked the court for time to review some things before he brought another set of questions to the prosecution's lineup. Judge Greene gave him five minutes.

Even though the white men were all pretending it hadn't happened, the trauma of that night in jail away from her children and her husband would follow Ella every waking minute for the rest of her life.

The Ranchers

Something had been bothering Jewell throughout the day. *What were these well-to-do white men doing in here? Why would they spend an entire day sitting with black people when the majority of white spectators had made it a point not to be anywhere near the blacks?*

During Jesse's five minutes, Jewell decided she'd go find out. They looked like a bunch of ranchers to her.

Sidling up to the pew where the group was sitting, Jewell took a seat. She asked them what had brought them to court on a nice day like this.

What they said stunned her. They were very interested in this case because they wanted to see what would happen to the sheriff and his men. One rancher leaned forward and said he was sick of his black workers being beaten up every time they came to town. Another volunteered that one of his black employees had been dragged down the street with a rope. If the workers had anything at all to drink, they would be beaten up. The men wanted to see if justice would be done to the sheriff and his men.

The gentleman beside Jewell reiterated that their employees couldn't walk on the sidewalk, use the public toilets, get a cup of coffee, or anything else in Macon.

The row of men nodded in agreement.

That was a reassuring little exchange, Jewell thought. Here, she and Bryce had believed that nearly every white person in the county were mean to black people, but these men wanted to stand up against Farrar and his posse. She felt somewhat better about Noxubee County.

As for the lawmen, Jewell happened to recognize the same deputy she'd ignored out in the parking lot at the bond hearing a year ago.

The officers were twitching around with their guns and things in the courtroom, wanting everyone to see that they were armed, Jewell speculated.

She and the officer from the parking lot picked up where they had left off.

He said, "We're going to send your niggers up. They're going to be on the rock pile."

She said, "Huh? You're not sending my friends anyplace, you little turd. I grew up in the Hatfield and McCoy territory."

He put his hand on his gun.

She said, "You talk about shooting? That would make them laugh up a storm to see your puny gun where I'm from. You talk about shooting? I'll meet you down in the yard, and we'll have a duel. Then we'll see who can shoot."

The gavel sounded in perfect time.

Wrap-Up

Jesse called Emmett Farrar back to the stand.

The witness elaborated in great detail on the hand motions Ella had engaged in regarding her handbag and her gun, even going so far as to show about how far the fingers of her right hand had reached into the bag before he stopped her.

Citing Farrar's justice court testimony, Jesse pressed for an exact chronology of whether Nelse had already been under arrest when Ella approached the sheriff. This was necessary to prove whether or not she had actually tried to interfere with an officer during a pending arrest.

"I am trying to tell it as near right as I know how, Mr. Stennis. I am under oath. I can't remember everything word for word, but I have no reason to lie about this thing," Farrar pleaded.

"Now, if Your Honor please, there is no insinuation that this man is lying, and I certainly want the record to show what I am trying to do is not insinuate about anything but get the facts to these gentlemen who are going to have to pass on this case," Jesse responded.

"All right. Any further questions?" Judge Greene said.

"Yes, sir," Jesse said, and he moved in.

"I will ask you, Mr. Sheriff, if when you testified in justice court you were not asked this question then: 'Do you tell this court and jury that she ever attempted to put her hand in that purse in your presence?' and that you then replied, 'I have never told anyone that.' And you said further that 'I understand that you,' speaking to me, 'have talked a whole lot about it but I have never once said she went in the purse.' I will ask you if you said that under your oath in justice court?" Jesse asked.

Farrar attempted to answer the question by explaining himself. Jesse objected. The judge agreed.

By direction of Judge Greene, Jesse read from the justice court transcript, revealing that Farrar had in fact denied that Ella had reached into her purse. So much for intimidating an officer.

On this day, Stennis eventually elicited from the deputy sheriff, "I don't remember telling anyone that I said that she never attempted to put her hand in the purse, Judge."

Jesse recalled R. L. Richardson. Richardson categorically denied his justice court testimony where he had said Ella had pulled her purse away from Farrar and that Farrar had grabbed it and opened it.

Jesse requested to confer with Harpole Patterson, the court reporter who'd recorded the justice court testimony. The judge first wanted to know if the state rested. It did.

Immediately, the state made a motion to reopen in order to introduce records. Judge Greene dismissed the jurors and granted the motion.

Incredulous, Jesse rose to his feet. He wouldn't agree to the filing of any records at this stage. The judge insisted. Jesse objected. The judge overruled, advising that the state just wanted to introduce some records. "What records?" Jesse wanted to know.

"The affidavit, the warrant, and the bond, and the Sheriff's return on the warrant, not the judgment," Lucas responded.

Jesse took a deep breath.

"I want to make a motion here. Comes the defendant and moves the Court to exclude the evidence and direct the jury to find the Defendant not guilty, for the reason that the State has wholly failed to prove by competent evidence the guilt of the Defendant as charged in the affidavit and for the further reason that proper jurisdiction of this court has not been shown as required by law and for the further reason that the affidavit charges that Nelse Gaston was being arrested for driving while under the influence of an intoxicant and the testimony shows that Nelse Gaston was arrested on the charge of reckless driving and there is therefore a material variance between the charge as set out in the affidavit and the testimony as offered in behalf of the State of Mississippi."

"Well, overruled," Judge Greene answered. "The motion will be overruled. Let the jury come out."

Jesse looked at the ceiling.

Buck interjected that he didn't think Jesse had the right to make a motion until the State rested.

Miss Bell, bewildered, asked what the record should show. The judge instructed that it should show that the State rested, made a motion to reopen, and introduced certain records. "Leave it right where it is," he ordered.

For good measure, Jesse put Farrar back on the stand, which gave the defense an opportunity to nail down his contradictory testimonies. The chief deputy testified that he didn't remember charging Nelse with reckless driving. Farrar and others had testified that Nelse's arrest was for that particular infraction.

For the first time during the hearing, Brown stood to defend Farrar, complaining to the bench that Farrar should be allowed to explain himself. So the deputy sheriff testified that Nelse was not arrested for reckless driving but was charged with driving under the influence of intoxicating liquor.

Finally, the State really did rest.

Jesse renewed his motion for preemptory instruction and assigned as grounds the reasons stipulated in his lengthy previous motion. The fact that the State had failed to file the records seemed to be a fatal flaw in its case because there was no case without the documents. It was not as though the date of the trial had been a secret.

Overruled.

So appeared the amount of care given to legal accuracy for the charges filed against black people in 1960 Noxubee County.

The defense called Harpole Patterson for the purpose of attesting to his transcript.

Directing the court reporter to rely on his transcription for answers, Stennis asked if patrolman Richardson had previously testified that there had been a scuffle between the sheriff and Ella. He had not. Jesse asked if Deputy Hutcherson had testified that Nelse had laughed at him. He had not.

Harpole confirmed that the sheriff had testified that Nelse was initially arrested for reckless driving, and he testified that he had never once said Ella had gone into her purse.

Lucas objected, asserting that Jesse had been putting words in the witness's mouth.

Jesse replied that predicate had been laid out to allow the line of questioning.

The senator countered, "Now you can lay out your predicate. That is very true, you can lay your predicate, but you can't start at the outer skins of his teeth and go plumb down into his stomach, run your elbow plumb down into his craw and draw the answer out, like has been drawn here."

This exchange was certainly the kind of entertainment courthouse gawkers enjoyed.

Jesse resignedly asked Harpole to read directly from the justice of the peace transcripts.

Lucas, for the State on cross, countered that just because no one had testified previously about Nelse laughing or Ella putting her hand in her purse didn't mean that it hadn't occurred.

Jesse maintained that Patterson was a witness called solely to contradict previous testimony and that asking him about anything else would yield incompetent evidence.

Undeterred, Lucas pressed on, asking the court reporter to read various bits and pieces of justice court testimony.

Jesse continued objecting as to burdening the record with incompetent evidence.

Overruled.

A couple of questions and answers later, Jesse again rose to object. "We would like to interpose our objection here for the record that this is not in cross-examination of this witness's direct testimony and this witness was put on for the sole purpose of contradicting the fact that the witness, Hutcherson, testified under his oath here that he did tell the court and jury in justice court that there was a scuffle between the sheriff and the defendant, Ella Gaston."

"All right, objection sustained," the judge ruled. "I am going to stop this. I don't think it's necessary anyway."

Lucas's questioning and Patterson's reading barreled forward, nevertheless. Jesse shook his head and stared at his yellow pad. He'd given up taking notes.

Jesse eventually prevailed with his objection that the cross-examination testimony was venturing off into areas not addressed during direct examination.

Judge Greene sustained the objection again and then allowed Lucas to read "two more lines" from the transcript anyway.

Jesse was beyond incredulous. The State was now contradicting itself from the witness stand.

"This is a contradiction of the State's testimony by its witness, Richardson, and we object to going into any further into the record as it would only serve to burden the record, and it is incompetent," Jesse said, stating what he thought was the obvious.

"Overruled. Objection overruled. I don't think it is competent anywhere. Go ahead and read it."

So the senator continued to draw testimony in contradiction to the State's own case.

On redirect, Jesse queried Harpole about testimony that underscored it was indeed the sheriff who had opened the purse by citing Richardson's justice court statements.

What the jury heard meant that the scenario claiming Ella had approached the sheriff with her hand down in her purse was only recently added to the arrest narrative. Painting Ella as overtly threatening the sheriff with a gun was the key component of the State's charge that she had intimidated an officer. Whether this revelation made any difference to the panel or not, it was hard to tell, but at least it was on record.

Next up for the defense was Bryce McMahan.

Among questions asked to establish Bryce's identity and trustworthiness, including his profession, service on the board of education, being a deacon at the Baptist church, and helping with his wife's nursing home, Jesse took the opportunity to engage in a small game of "Name That Neighbor" for jurors' benefit.

"We had a lady here named Miss McMahan, who taught school in our—taught school here in Macon for a number of years, married Mr. Frank Hurst. You related to her?"

"She was my cousin."

And so the jurors, some of whom may have been students of Miss McMahan, were drawn to observe the witness in perhaps a more favorable light.

Bryce testified that Ella had worked for the Hattiesburg Convalescent Center for approximately four years and that her reputation in the community for peace and violence was "Very excellent. She is respected both by the Negro people—"

Senator Lucas interrupted, "Now we submit, if Your Honor please, he is not answering it."

"Only two ways to answer it—either good or bad," Judge Greene advised.

"Very excellent," Bryce repeated.

The senator took up the questioning on cross-examination.

"You feel a very keen interest in the welfare of your servants, do you not?"

"I would like to see justice done to them, I surely would."

"I didn't ask you about justice now. That is a matter that is up to somebody beside you."

"Yes, I realize that."

After establishing that Bryce had made at least six trips to Noxubee in the interest of the case, Lucas asked if, even in the face of evidence indicating that Ella had tried to pull a pistol on the sheriff, "Do you still tell this jury that her reputation for peace and violence is good?"

"I certainly do."

"Yes, sir, that is all then."

Bryce turned to the jury.

"I most certainly do."

On redirect, Jesse asked Bryce to elaborate on why he had such an interest in the defendant's case. The senator objected, and the judge ruled:

Now gentlemen, really as a matter of law, under the rules of evidence, you can't go into a lot of this. Just ask them whether they know the reputation or not and whether it is good or bad. Of course, I think in this case it is well to show this man's standing down there, but that is the end of it. You can't go into any details and objection will be sustained. You may stand down.

Jewell was the final witness.

Jesse led her through the usual identification questioning. She testified that she was married to Bryce, and they'd been married since 1942. She told the jurors that Ella had been employed at the nursing home as head cook since January 1956.

Jewell testified that Ella had not missed a day of work for seven months prior to her February 1959 trip to Shuqualak to check on her ailing mother-in-law.

"I will ask you, Mrs. McMahan, if you will tell this court and jury whether or not you know Ella Gaston's general reputation for peace and violence in the community in which she lives and resides?" Jesse asked.

"Yes, sir, I do."

"Would you turn to the jury and tell these men whether it is good or bad?" he continued.

"It is excellent."

The State declined cross-examination. The woman had already made it clear she was completely unafraid to say what she thought, and who knew what that would be.

The Defense rested.

The jurors filed out to allow the attorneys time to prepare closing arguments.

Jesse kept launching missiles.

First, he asked the judge to instruct the jury to find the defendant not guilty based on "material variance between the affidavit and the testimony and for the additional reason that the uncontradicted proof is that Nelse Gaston had already been placed under arrest before the defendant ever got out of the automobile and before the defendant had ever spoken a word." In other words, Ella couldn't have obstructed Nelse's arrest if he was already arrested before she got out of the car.

"The motion will be overruled," Judge Greene ruled.

Next, Jesse asked for closing arguments to be taken down by Miss Bell in the same manner as the judge had allowed the opening arguments to be recorded.

"The motion will be overruled."

Judge Greene did allow court rulings made during the arguments to be recorded along with any objections.

Jesse began objecting to all three prosecution attorneys' participating in closing arguments.

Senator Lucas interrupted opposing counsel midsentence: "Ain't but two of us going to argue it."

"Gentlemen, let me get my objection in the record, Bill. Comes the defendant—"

Judge Greene interjected, "Let the jury come out."

Jesse continued, "… and objects to—Can I make this motion in the absence of the jury, Your Honor?"

"Well, you can make it, Jesse, but it is absolutely unnecessary. I never heard of a motion like that being made. The court has already ruled that can't but two speak."

The judge stated to the assembly that the defense had wanted thirty minutes and the State had wanted twenty minutes, and he would split the difference, giving both parties twenty-five minutes to present closing arguments. Then jurors heard last pleas from both sides in the misdemeanor case that had riveted a packed courtroom for a solid day.

Instructions

Jury instructions are normally provided to the judge by both sides in the case, and in the introduction of the instruction, the judge announces on whose behalf the instruction is given.

For example, *Instruction VI* said, "The Court instructs the jury for the defendant, Ella Gaston, that it is just as much your duty under the law and upon your oaths to turn a person aloose by your verdict of 'Not guilty' as it is for you to convict a guilty one."

In all, Judge Greene issued thirteen separate jury instructions, among them for the State: if the jurors believed beyond a reasonable doubt and to a moral certainty that Ella had placed herself between the Sheriff and her husband during his impending arrest and that she tried to get a pistol out of her purse trying to impede and intimidate the Sheriff, they should find her guilty. Further, Greene advised the jurors, for the State, that even though they'd heard Ella had a good character, their belief in her guilt should result in a verdict of guilty.

Significantly, the Judge refused to issue one jury instruction:

> Instruction No. I–The Court instructs the jury for the defendant that, before you can convict this defendant, the State of Mississippi must convince your minds by competent evidence beyond a reasonable doubt that the defendant threatened the prosecution officer, Mr. Emmett Farrar, and that, in addition thereto, impeded and persuaded him from the performance of a lawful duty, and that vague, intemperate language, if such were used, without apparent purpose is not sufficient. A. J. Vol. 39, p. 508.

Jewell and Ella had barely enough time to return from the whites-only ladies' room when it was announced that the jury had a verdict. As expected, the foreman's note said they'd found Ella guilty as charged. Apparently, "as charged" turned out to be "attempting to intimidate and impede an officer in the performance of his duty." At least that's what her appearance bond stated. It wasn't on the jury's declaration paper. It had been difficult to pinpoint the actual charge since she'd been sent to circuit court with papers from the justice of the peace court declaring she was guilty of "obstructing justice."

Her attorney asked for the jury to be polled. Each man reported his vote as "guilty."

Jesse immediately put the court on notice that his client intended to file an appeal to the Mississippi Supreme Court.

Unperturbed, Judge Greene ordered Ella to serve four months in the county jail at hard labor and pay a fine of $250 including all costs in the case. Further, he ordered a $1,000 appeal bond if Ella wanted to stay out of jail during the appeal.

Ella's lawyer was suddenly busy making pronouncements concerning the appeal process, bonds to keep her out of jail, and various other motions laid before the court to ensure that his client wouldn't be hauled off from the courtroom as a convict. He had been well prepared for this eventuality.

It was all just chatter to Jewell. She looked at Bryce and said, "Doesn't matter. Ella will never be in a jail or in a courtroom again. I can promise you that."

Safe Travels

The courtroom began to clear out, Judge Greene had departed, and people were milling around in the second-floor lobby. Deputy Sheriff Farrar, whose wife was the statutory keeper of the courthouse, was holding sway downstairs, glad-handing, and slapping the backs of his fellow officers.

A more jubilant crowd rarely had been observed following a misdemeanor trial.

Bill and his rider left for Hattiesburg. The rest of the Gaston team stayed in their places. Jesse stepped over to Circuit Clerk J. E. McDavid and asked for a private meeting room so he could confer with his clients before they left for Hattiesburg.

"Sorry. Locked up," McDavid said. The clerk made a hasty retreat out the back door and down the hall toward the back stairs.

Jesse was hard on his heels. He stopped at the frosted glass door of a witness room and checked the doorknob. It was loose. Slipping unnoticed into the room, which overlooked the back parking lot, Jesse checked for occupants. There weren't any. This would make a fine meeting place, he reasoned. He stepped over to survey the parking lot and stopped dead in his tracks.

It didn't take much to tell that the white men lurking around the Hattiesburg cars meant no good to anyone. They were casual about it, all right. Leaning against the trees, quietly smoking cigarettes, they were intently watching the back door of the courthouse. Across the street in front of the ancient jailhouse, a couple of others were sitting way back in a pickup truck with its motor running, windows open. Their hats were pulled down to the side. It was hard to make out their faces in the gloom.

Still in the courtroom, the Gastons, McMahans, and their friends from Forrest County were busy recounting all the errors they'd heard in testimony that afternoon. Jesse briskly interrupted the recapitulation.

"Back here," he said, motioning from a door behind the bench. "Y'all need to come back here. Now. I've found us a meeting room."

The group hustled down the narrow hall behind the courtroom and into the small witness room.

"Now, we need to talk strategy, but I've got to run across to my office and get something first," Jesse explained. "I'll be just a minute."

He surreptitiously locked the door behind him. They could hear his footsteps pounding quick and heavy on the linoleum floor of the hall and down the stairs. The group resumed their analyses.

Bryce cracked the back window and lit a cigarette. There had been plenty of cigarette smoke in the courtroom–the judge had even puffed on a cigar–but Bryce had refrained from smoking inside the building. For some reason it didn't seem right to him. It would be like smoking in school or church or something. He didn't feel right leaving the others to go outside, so he just hoped they'd indulge him a single cigarette. The ashtray in the room was already full.

Bryce's large, smoking silhouette backlit against the window panes created a nice target, the man below in the sweat-stained gray fedora thought. He made a little gun with his hand and pulled the trigger.

Ella focused on the fact that her jailers had gotten away with lying on the stand. The group discussed it at length. Everyone knew she had spent the night in jail. Why hadn't Jesse called them on this provable perjury? Ella told her friends she could hardly stand to sit still in that courtroom and listen to the lies. As for Nelse, his case was dragging along behind Ella's. He wondered out loud if they'd just continue his case forever.

Soon enough Jesse returned with a file in his hand. He never looked at it again.

Jesse again explained to the group what the strategy would be. He'd file a motion to the circuit court for a new trial, which would be denied. Jesse would next send a brief to the Supreme Court in a bid to overturn the verdict.

Against all odds, Jesse had faith that the all-white male appeals panel would see holes in the evidence and no truth in the charges, and they would throw out the case. Some of the men had been serving for a long time. All of them were smart. Jesse believed in the rule and sanctity of the law, and he honestly thought the justices felt the same way, he assured the group. What had happened in the courtroom today bore little resemblance to how a criminal case should be prosecuted, he asserted as a former district attorney.

Jesse said the best they could hope for was an overturning of the verdict. Next best would be a reversal and remand, which would mean they'd have to try the case again. The worst thing would be if the justices refused to hear the appeal. That would mean it would be all over in state court.

"Well, there's a higher court than that one, isn't there?" Jewell demanded.

"Yes, there are the federal courts," Jesse said.

"We'll just go to the feds, then, if this doesn't go our way," she said. "Ella will never go to jail again. And you know what else? She'll never stand trial again either."

Damn, this woman is obstinate, Jesse thought. The prosecution knew what they were doing when they didn't cross-examine her. She would have fried their ears.

Jesse didn't argue with her, though. Rather, he explained to them what the cost of an appeal to the Supreme Court would be.

Bryce and Jewell were ready. He pulled out an envelope of cash from his jacket pocket and handed it to the lawyer.

Nelse paid his own retainer for continuing the reckless driving or driving while intoxicated case pending against him, whichever they decided on. He and Jesse took a minute to speculate on how Nelse's charge would play out against Ella's.

While the lawyer and his client dissected that issue and the two women harrumphed about the arrest testimony, Bryce stepped back over to the window for a second smoke. *What the heck*, he told himself. *One more won't hurt.*

He pulled out his Zippo lighter, clicked it open, and stopped midway to the cigarette. Two highway patrol cruisers, coming from two different directions, had suddenly descended onto the back parking lot, red lights raging.

"Hey, what's this!" he said as the others began to notice the pulse of red against the interior walls of the tiny room. The group charged the window.

"That's your escort," Jesse said from behind them. "It's just safer this way."

"Y'all need to come on now," Jesse advised. "This way." He bustled them down the escape route and out the back door to their cars.

Bryce recognized one of the patrol officers. He'd been in the justice court bond hearing, but he hadn't testified today. Bryce nodded. The officer nodded back.

The fellas out under the tree just shrugged their shoulders and picked their teeth as they strode off to Jefferson Street. Suddenly, the night was much less entertaining. The driver of the waiting pickup raced his engine in the mechanical version of an obscene gesture.

And so the Hattiesburg company swept out of Macon flanked front and rear by highway patrol cars in a grand show of power.

In the parking lot, Jesse stood big and silent with his briefcase in his hand until every last person had cleared the yard and environs. Then he walked around the building, glanced over to the warmly lit first-floor quarters of the jail, and strode across the street to his little white office where another big issue was waiting in line after Ella's.

A month before, Jesse had been handed one of the most sensational murder cases to ever hit the area—the Gene Tate murder case up in Columbus. Jesse was defending Mississippi State College student Jon Mattox, the victim's handsome next-door neighbor, who had been arrested for the Sunday morning murder of the young mother of three. One of her sons had found her laid out dead in the garage, garroted with a coat hanger. Mrs. Tate was an up-and-coming society matron in the sedate and pretty antebellum town.

Judge Greene was the judge for that case too. Filing this Gaston appeal would not sit well with the old fellow, Jesse knew. But he wouldn't represent one client based on another's issue. If anything, Jesse knew how to compartmentalize his cases. He'd just let what happened happen. Some things you simply couldn't control.

He sat down and began sketching out Ella's motion for a new trial. There was a lot of material to choose from.

The Trip Home

The escorting troopers canned their red lights outside Macon but kept close to their charges. The departure scene should have been warning enough to any Klan thugs out for a good time, the officers reasoned, but they wanted to ensure that the group they were guarding made it to Meridian safe and sound.

Charlie Staten had the utmost respect for Jesse Stennis; plus, he'd watched the arrest of the Gastons almost a year ago. He was happy to help.

Jewell McMahan, the gun-toting, fearless Kentucky mountain woman, was suddenly aware of just how perilous this situation was. Having an unannounced highway patrol escort got her attention.

"We're really in a lot of danger," she said to Bryce under her breath. "I knew it was bad, but I didn't have any idea how bad until they showed up."

The McMahans and Gastons decided to stop at the Red Hot Truck Stop for supper. Jewell was in first.

"Look," she told the owner. "We've just come from Macon, and we have some colored friends with us. We're all hungry, and we want to eat here."

She waited for a negative response.

"Sure," the owner said. "Come back here. I'll show you the dining room we have for the Negroes."

She followed, imagining the worst, and skeptical that any such "dining room" existed. Most eating establishments, if they let blacks eat under the roof at all, provided a table or two in the kitchen.

What he proudly showed her was a large dining room, nicely decorated and fully appointed. "We don't believe in how things are done here, but we can't change it by ourselves," he said. "The least we can do is make sure where coloreds eat is just as nice as where whites eat."

By this time, the patrolmen were gone, and Bryce, Ella, and Nelse were standing just inside the cafe door.

Now there was another dilemma.

"Okay, there's a really nice dining room in the back," Jewell told them. "We'll eat back there with you, or you can eat by yourselves if you want to be alone to talk, or we'll all just sit down up here."

Ella and Nelse looked at each other. They'd be home on Lee Street with a house full of jubilant children shortly. Maybe they ought to take this opportunity to discuss the day's events as a married couple, off the public stage.

None of them had the energy to try to buck the system at this point. At least these people were aware the system was wrong.

"Thank you. We'll eat in the back," Nelse said.

Jewell and Ella scurried to the ladies' room. Neither of them noticed if there was a "Whites Only" sign on the door.

Mobile Street

Nine days later, *Sepia* magazine published the first installment of John Howard Griffin's *Black Like Me*, his journalistic foray into the world of the black community as a white man who'd undergone a skin color change. The release caused a nationwide commotion. For the first time, someone who wasn't born black was reporting in unvarnished splendor the realities of living "colored" in the Deep South.

The old racial mixing pot of New Orleans wasn't spared critical exposure as Griffin recounted the wearying task of trying to find a bathroom as a black man in the French Quarter. He found himself going into the back doors of restaurants to eat and training himself not to look in the faces of the white people he encountered, especially women.

Alabama also came under uncompromising scrutiny when Griffin hitchhiked from Mobile to Montgomery and encountered the vicarious curiosity of white men seeking first-hand knowledge about the sexual lives of black men. One particularly enthusiastic driver even asked the appalled Griffin to show his penis so the inquiring youth could see if it was, in fact, as big as he'd been told.

Met by silence, the curious one blurted out, "I wasn't going to do anything to you. I'm not a queer or anything." Griffin shrugged it off. One thing he'd learned as a black man: the sex life of the African American male was greatly exaggerated.

But no place described in the saga looked any worse than Mississippi. In one chapter, Griffin and others were riding in the back of a public bus en route to Mississippi from New Orleans. There was a ten-minute rest stop inside the Mississippi state line at one of the little towns along the way. The driver refused to let his black passengers off the bus to use the restroom.

I sat in the monochrome gloom of dusk, scarcely believing that in this year of freedom any man could deprive another of anything so basic as the need to quench thirst or use the restroom. There was nothing of the feel of America here. It was rather some strange country suspended in ugliness. Tension hung in the air, a continual threat, even though you could not put your finger on it.

From the back of a barbecue joint in full nighttime swing on Mobile Street in Hattiesburg, Griffin called for rescue by P. D. East, the rabble-rousing white newspaper editor from Petal. Griffin's depression caused by the realities of black life in the Hub City had overcome his determination to stay there. Griffin and East had known each other as journalists. Griffin trusted his colleague. East showed up late that night in the area few whites frequented unless they were looking for trouble. The author was never so glad to catch a ride, though he was hesitant to get in the front seat. He was black, after all.

East had gained local infamy for himself by taking on the Citizens' Council in print and picture in the *Petal Paper*. East had published a most infamous full-page ad in August 1956. It pictured a big-mouthed, singing donkey with the header, "Suh, Here's Sweet Music! Yes, YOU too, can be SUPERIOR. Join The Glorious Citizen's Clan Next Thursday Night!"

When *Time* Magazine picked up Griffin's story in March, white Hattiesburg was in an uproar. They were outraged at the portrayal of the black section of their town, where their general observation was that everyone was happy and had a great time, particularly at night. To have their joyful illusion shattered on the national stage by an "outsider" was galling.

However, Griffin's assessment of being black in Hattiesburg during his dismal moments on Mobile Street was far different:

> The laughter had to be gross or it would turn to sobs, and to sob would be to realize, and to realize would be to despair. So the noise poured forth like a jazzed-up fugue, louder and louder to cover the whisper in every man's soul. "You are black. You are condemned." This is what the white man mistook for "jubilant living" and called "whooping it up."

Bryce's lifelong effort in Hattiesburg was as someone who had worked closely with blacks, respected, encouraged, and defended them. He was profoundly disheartened that despite his own personal efforts, his hometown was being painted to look so awful to the nation.

So he picked up the phone and called P. D. East.

"I need to see you," Bryce told the newspaperman, who by now was accustomed to getting irate phone calls from white men.

"I mean you no harm," Bryce said. "I just don't believe it's this bad. I want you to help me correct this. It's hurting every person in this town–black and white. We need to fix this."

East agreed to meet with the insistent real estate developer.

And so, Bryce the Fixer was off on another mission, this time to put right the outrageous claims against Hattiesburg perpetrated by East's friend, this writer from Texas.

He came back from that visit a very disappointed man.

That was about the time Bryce quietly started donating to the local NAACP chapter. It wasn't anything he expected or wanted to be publicly known; supporting that organization was, after all, a proven risk to one's business. When he became chapter chair, though, J. C. Fairley made sure his members knew.

The McMahans enjoyed a particularly robust friendship with their black acquaintances, and their sons thought everyone lived that way.

ELLA GASTON V.
STATE OF MISSISSIPPI

The Appellant

Jesse's plate was full. He had Ella's appeal to prepare and the other important case waiting in the wings. Ella's appeal would not wait, though, even for the glamorous Gene Tate murder case.

During Ella's trial, Jesse had kept a running list of what he perceived to be reversible errors. It was long. As a first volley for Ella's appeal, Jesse had laid out twenty detailed reasons in his February 18 motion for a new trial showing why his client, now Appellant Gaston, believed the case should be reversed. The move was a necessary precursor to filing an appeal to the Supreme Court.

The appellant's motion was not kind to the judge, and he ruled against it. Consequently, Ella would exercise her right to have her case heard before the highest court in the state with all attendant allegations against Greene's judicial performance aired out in broad public record. So be it.

A month or so later, up in Columbus, Jesse Stennis was battling it out in Judge Greene's local courtroom on behalf of his young client, Jon Mattox. By this time, Jon had become somewhat of a celebrity, and the notion that he'd engaged in a prolonged affair with the older, beautiful, and married Gene Tate only added to his charisma. The courtroom was being flooded by swooning students from the local Mississippi State College for Women as well as enthralled coeds from Mississippi State.

The whole production was being carried live via radio, and a large contingent of print journalists was on hand to record every breathless moment of what some viewed as the most thrilling murder trial in state history. At one point, the upstairs courtroom became so crowded that office workers below feared the floor above them would cave in. Efforts to quell attendance failed. Everyone just hoped for the best.

As for the strained relationship between the defense attorney and the judge, attendees reported that whenever Jesse would stand to object, address the court, or examine a witness, Judge Greene would completely turn his back to the courtroom. Only when Jesse stood down would the jurist turn back to face onlookers, much of the time through a cloud of cigar smoke.

If the Mattoxes believed this did not portend well for their son, no one was aware. They had hired the preeminent defense attorney in the area, after all.

It had taken a while for Miss Bell to get the Gaston trial transcription finished. On May 2, she'd asked for a thirty-day extension. Like Jesse, she had been enmeshed in the Gene Tate affair, which had not turned out well for the defendant. Miss Bell was busily working up the transcript from that case for the appeal process too. For transcribing her shorthand notes and being in court for the Gaston trial on February 17, Miss Bessie Kate presented a bill of $93.52 to the court for 19,250 words at twenty-five cents per hundred words as allowed by law, a $1.50 binding fee, a $2.00 express fee, a $1.00 filing fee, a $1.00 approving bond fee, and a $39.90 court reporter cost fee. She'd finished the project on May 27.

Under client orders that the Gastons were not to appear in the Noxubee courtroom again, on August 17, Jesse managed to secure a dismissal of Ella's concealed weapon charge, though she had to pay court costs. On the same day, Nelse paid the $125 fine for driving a motor vehicle while under the influence of intoxicating liquor levied upon him by Justice of the Peace Woodfin, even though Nelse was charged with reckless driving. Those two things were out of the way.

By September 3, Jesse was ready for Ella's appeal. His first filing to the Supreme Court was the Assignment of Errors, listing thirteen reasons why the Justices should reverse the lower court's decision:

1. The court and jury had erred in their findings of facts and conclusion of law.
2. The verdict and sentence were contrary to the overwhelming weight of evidence.
3. Prosecuting witnesses' testimonies varied greatly from what they'd said in justice court.

The remaining assertions were aimed directly at the court's performance. Appellant maintained that Judge Greene

4. erred when he denied Ella's motion for a directed verdict of not guilty;
5. erred when he denied Ella's motion for a new trial;
6. erred by making many prejudicial statements and side remarks in the presence of the jury;
7. erred by denying both of Ella's motions for a directed verdict of not guilty;
8. erred by allowing all of the State's jury instructions;
9. erred by refusing any of Ella's jury instructions;

10. erred by permitting testimony that Ella had attempted to prevent Nelse's arrest when it had already happened for an offense with which he'd never been charged;

11. erred by overruling Ella's motion to quash the affidavit in August;

12. erred by overruling Ella's demurrer to the affidavit; and

13. erred by allowing evidence that Nelse was drunk.

Accompanying the assignment of errors was the brief for appellant, an eighteen-page discussion expounding on the most damning assertions in the thirteen-item list. Jesse described the errant rulings, testimony, and comments in detail, pulling in direct quotes from the case transcript and calling the Justices' attention to Judge Greene's frequent inexplicable remarks such as admitting to "letting in a lot of incompetent proof."

Significantly, Jesse proposed that when Judge Greene allowed Farrar and his former deputy to testify that the Gastons were arrested during a manhunt for a Negro who had attacked a white marshal, the judge allowed the jurors' minds to be infused with racial prejudice.

> The learned Circuit Judge permitted the State, in its opening statement to the jury, to bring out the fact that an officer of the Town of Shuqualak had been molested by a Negro on the previous night, that is to say the night previous to the stopping of Nelse Gaston, and his arrest on a charge of reckless driving. ... In that same opening statement, the court permitted the State to bring out again that Mr. Moore, the officer of the Town of Shuqualak, had been attacked by a negro, and that the negro

was related to this appellant. In addition to this, the
court permitted the State to introduce testimony,
over the objection of the defense, about this same
situation. The only purpose that this kind of thing
could possibly serve would be to inflame the minds
of a Mississippi white jury against the appellant,
because it indirectly brings in the racial question,
and indirectly connects the appellant with a negro
who had made an attack, allegedly, on an officer of
the Town of Shuqualak. The sheriff testified about
this over the objection of the defense, as shown by
page 47 of the record. This same matter was referred
to by Chief Deputy Sheriff Hutcherson, as shown
on page 53.

Jesse asserted that allowing officers to speak of finding a .22 rifle,
which had no bearing on the charges against Ella, was also an act
that would have prejudiced the jury against his client.

Further, "The verdict in this case is contrary to the overwhelming
weight of the believable testimony, and the conviction was brought
about largely by prejudicial testimony and other errors prejudicial to
this appellant's interests and rights."

Jesse chose to argue from the position that Ella had not been
arrested on February 22 at all, as the officers had sworn. And, in
fact, the Sheriff's affidavit had not been sworn to until February 24.
Thus, he maintained, his client had not been properly arrested. He
himself had gotten her out of the jail on February 23, although that
wasn't part of the record.

Jesse closed the body of the brief with a discussion on the matter
of Nelse allegedly slinging loose gravel on the sheriff and his men.
He wrote,

Driving in loose gravel or over muddy roads, or even on narrow country roads, to many of us has become a lost art, especially with an automobile powered by a 200 horsepower engine. It is very easy for a person accustomed to driving on pavement to spin his wheels in loose gravel. The sheriff took it as a personal affront, by the uncontradicted testimony in this case. And, had not the loose gravel been at the place where Nelse Gaston started from Dorroh Hill in the presence of the sheriff and his special deputy, Nelse Gaston and his wife and grandchildren would have gone on back to their home in Hattiesburg, Mississippi.

As a parting plea, Jesse stated what was obvious to the defense team.

"In submitting this Brief, we would like to state with all of the frankness and sincerity at our control that this appellant was convicted because the sheriff and his deputies and assistants made up their minds that they were going to convict her, regardless of what it took on their part. And the Court would certainly be justified in reversing this decision and judgement and sentence and releasing the appellant."

With the appellant brief filed, the Attorney General's Office, representing the State of Mississippi, now took a run at knocking down the appeal. On board for Attorney General Joe T. Patterson was G. Garland Lyell, Jr., assistant attorney general and crack defender of the "Southern Way of Life."

Lyell's response in *Ella Gaston v. State of Mississippi* recounted the State's version of the narrative that led to the Gastons' arrest, including the assertion that the couple had "six or eight Negro children piled hurriedly into the car" as it "took off at a high rate of speed down the road." The timeline also included Nelse's immediate arrest by the sheriff for reckless driving, after which Ella entered the scene with a large handbag in her left hand and her "fingers having gotten down into the bag" when the sheriff snatched the purse and discovered the pistol.

Perhaps unconsciously, Lyell had proven Jesse's contention that if Nelse's arrest had already been made, Ella couldn't have interfered with it.

Lyell asserted that the affidavit was worded well enough to stand the test that Ella had indeed obstructed justice and that "her actions amounted to an assault" even though there wasn't a mention in the affidavit of Ella reaching inside her purse and coming out with a gun.

He did admit that there were two charges levied against Nelse, but that the difference between reckless driving and driving while intoxicated were not material enough "to be considered harmful."

Lyell addressed Ella's contention that she was not properly arrested by invoking a "milk-of-human-kindness" explanation.

> The record plainly shows that the very valid reason
> for not putting her under arrest promptly at the time
> was that she had a car full of small Negro children
> and there was no one at the time with whom she
> could leave these children. Humanitarian instincts
> dictated that the woman be allowed freedom until
> she had time to turn this brood over to someone
> for caretaking.

As to the discrepancies in testimony between the justice court and the circuit court, Lyell had this to say: "Suffice it to say, it does not appear that there is any material variation other than normal variation between the manner in which any normal witness would testify from time to time about the same fact or circumstance. ... Their testimony in Circuit Court stands unimpeached."

On the matter of prejudicial remarks by the Court: "With deference to appellant's counsel, in every instance where perhaps prejudicial statements were made except one, the court promptly corrected the matter by sustaining an objection and instructing the jury to disregard it."

So, with admission that there was perhaps this "one" prejudicial statement in the record, Lyell filed his response on September 27 for the September term of court.

The wait began.

The Decision

Jesse knew his brief was late and the issue likely would not be addressed until November, depending on when the State responded. He got the copy of Lyell's response on October 1; it had been filed on September 27. That pretty much sealed it, Jesse decided. Nothing would be issued before November, and maybe it would be later than that. It wasn't unusual for appeals to languish in the court for months or even a year or more.

So when he got the call from a colleague that the decision was in the hand-downs on October 17, Jesse was stunned. No doubt, it was bad news–probably a cursory denial. This overcast Monday morning was a perfect setting for a depressing message.

Jesse asked the caller, a law school classmate, to go get a copy of the decision. He sat despondently by the phone waiting on the inevitable, making notes on how he'd break the news to the clients.

First, he knew Ella would indeed have to spend time in jail unless he could keep her out on bond while he appealed the case to the United States Supreme Court. Given that court's decisions over the past decade, he was reasonably certain that the outcome would be good. If he couldn't get her released on appeal bond, though, and she had to spend the time in jail, the unlikelihood of a fast-track decision from the federal bench would mean she'd wind up spending her entire sixty-day sentence behind bars anyway. A victory in Washington would be Pyrrhic.

Ella was a beautiful woman. He feared for her safety inside any jail. Who knew, after all of this, what "hard labor" would mean for her.

Then there was the boisterous Mrs. McMahan, who had vehemently declared that her friend would never spend another minute behind bars.

He dreaded this.

Then the call came.

Without any further input from either Jesse or Lyell, the Mississippi Supreme Court had reviewed the appeal and decided on its own that the lower court had indeed erred—on *grounds of allowing testimony that inserted the element of racial prejudice into the proceedings.* The failure of Judge Greene to sustain Jesse's objection to Farrar's testimony that there was a manhunt underway for "a Negro by the name of Frank Ed Hill" had struck a nerve with the high court. They ordered the case reversed and remanded on this point.

Writing for the Court, Presiding Justice William Etheridge also agreed with Jesse's assertions in other critical areas. The court recognized that evidence and contrary testimonies from justice court to circuit court did not support the affidavit charge that Ella intimidated or threatened an officer. They found that testimony allowed about the rifle found in the Gastons' car was irrelevant to the case at hand, and when Judge Greene denied Jesse's objection calling it incompetent proof, Judge Greene agreed that he had been "very liberal in letting in a lot of incompetent proof." Altogether, the Supreme Court had been less than kind to the circuit court judge's decision-making capabilities in this case. Chief Justice Elijah Harvey McGehee, C. J., and justices John William Kyle, Richard Olney Arrington, and Robert Gill Gillespie had concurred. There were no dissents.

The Announcement

Jesse contacted Bryce with the news. The impossible had occurred. The Supreme Court had agreed to reverse the decision. There was one problem: it was also remanded. That meant Ella would have to stand trial again. Just when it would be scheduled, no one knew.

Jesse said he thought the current bond would still stand, but Ella sure didn't need to come back to Noxubee before this next trial. And she needed to watch where she was going in Hattiesburg. Word traveled.

The two men arranged payment for the new trial before Bryce called Jewell.

Ella was in the kitchen preparing supper when she saw Jewell's Lincoln swooping down Lee Street. She washed and dried her hands and barely opened the door before Jewell would have knocked it down.

It took a minute for Ella to exactly absorb the message. They'd thrown out the old trial, and now they had to get ready for a new trial?

At once, she was filled with joy and dread. Rocking back and forth, she listened to her friend who was going on and on.

"You know they'll want you back in court. We'll do whatever we have to," Jewell reminded her. "You know we agreed that you would never, ever go back to court. We're going to figure something out, but we'll be happy today."

Jewell gave her a big, long hug and soared out the door.

Yes, we'll be happy, Ella thought. She could hardly wait for Nelse to get home. She was going to be happy today, for sure.

Ella looked up and raised her hand. "Thank you, Jesus. Thank you, Lord."

Up in Noxubee County, word was that the prosecution was stunned and surly. At first, they didn't believe it, but when the document finally arrived from Jackson, there was no denying it.

Judge Greene refused to comment to anyone about it, not even his clerks. In fact, the Gaston reversal was the first of three that would come back to him within the span of a few months.

Jon Mattox had been found guilty in March; Jesse appealed and gained a new trial for the defendant based on Greene's erroneous decision to admit testimony concerning a lie detector test.

Sandwiched between the Gaston trial in February and the Mattox affair in March was one of the nation's first lawsuits concerning the devastating effects of bug poisons being heavily used in Mississippi's Delta. Judge Greene had sat in as a special judge in the *Charles Lawler V. W. T. Skelton et al.* trial in Indianola. Lawler had been directly hit with poison by a crop duster and developed lifelong debilitating illness as a result. Dr. Mary Hogan, who had diagnosed pervasive chemical poisoning in Glen Allan in 1957 due to crop-dusting practices, was brought forward as plaintiff's expert witness. The court had sustained the defense's objection that Dr. Hogan's testimony would have been based on experiences from the 1957 case and barred her testimony. The Supreme Court deemed that decision a reversible error in May 1961.

In Hattiesburg, the Gastons and McMahans enjoyed their traditional rituals over Thanksgiving and Christmas. New Year's Eve had been celebrated on Lee Street and West Twenty-Fourth Street with sparklers, Roman candles, Black Cat fire crackers, and the occasional boom of an M-80.

Then they waited.

The Illness

The two women didn't know precisely what it would take to make sure that Ella never, ever set foot back in that fancy jail building as a prisoner, or back in the courtroom, for that matter, but they wanted options to delay and divert, if that time ever came. Jewell told Ella she had a thing or two up her sleeve that the yokels from Noxubee wouldn't anticipate–lots of handy connections in Hattiesburg. Ella and Jewell decided they'd shoot the moon and call them in.

The first was a young man in the district attorney's office. Jewell placed a call to him and invited him over to her office for a little chat. If there was anything Jewell McMahan knew how to do, it was make whoever was in her sights feel as though he or she were the center of the known universe. Jewell was mesmerizing like that. And she usually got her way, whatever it happened to be.

Jewell confided to the young prosecutor that she intended to move heaven and hell if necessary to keep her friend out of jail. Over a cup of coffee enjoyed in Jewell's sumptuous office, the young man agreed to let Jewell know when the Forrest County's DA office had communication with its counterpart in Noxubee County concerning the Gaston case. As a part of the deal, Jewell would never reveal his name. He kept his part of the pact, and she kept hers.

She placed a second call to her doctor, a gentlemanly, aristocratic New Orleans native who had moved north to practice family medicine. Not only was he Jewell's doctor, but he also attended several residents of her nursing home. She and Ella had figured out a way to keep the Farrar gang from laying another hand on Ella, Jewell confided to the physician, but she would need a trustworthy doctor to help them.

As an educated individual who was reared in the occasionally more casual racial blend of New Orleans, the doctor had been unprepared for the sheer weight of the fiercely segregated social structure dominating all of Mississippi culture, he told Jewell. The elegant doctor with impeccable manners would help the women in any way he could, he promised.

As Jewell and Ella refined the plot, they agreed that although it was dramatic, it would likely be the only way Ella could escape going back to jail, if things happened like Jesse kept saying they would. He was convinced the case would result in another guilty verdict.

Both of the women knew that what they planned was extremely dangerous and probably illegal.

The call came in to Jewell's office late on a Friday afternoon in January from her source in the district attorney's office. They'd received notice that a trial date had been set. She replaced the fancy receiver in its cradle and meditated on the message for a little while.

This was it.

She called the doctor. We have a court date, she reported, and started taking notes.

Then she called Ella and Bryce, in that order.

Jewell stepped out of her office and down the hall to the center's supply closet. Picking up a white laundry bag, she stuffed a number of red rubber hot-water bladders into it and took the package to her car.

With detailed instructions on what to purchase at the pharmacy, Jewell bought up the ingredients for the mixture that would safely render Ella into a dizzy, puking, miserable mess in no time.

Her next stop was Lee Street.

Jewell got out of the car with a white paper bag in her hand.

The two friends laughed nervously in Ella's kitchen as they mixed the potion. This was one of the boldest moves either of them had ever undertaken. The thought of that infernal jail and those horrid people spurred them forward.

The friends had decided months before that Ella would never go back, and this was the first salvo in the resistance.

Showtime

A couple of weeks later, things were progressing as normal in the Gaston and McMahan households. Saturday morning was filled with cartoons and the afternoon with playtime for the boys and hair time for the girls. The mothers gave their husbands a list of things to pick up during the obligatory Saturday trips "to town." On Sunday morning, church bustle was in full motion at both places, and, afterward, everyone reported to their respective homes for dinner—fried chicken for the Gastons and pot roast for the McMahans.

"I've gotta go," Jewell told her family as they settled in after lunch. "Ella's sick."

The boys looked at each other. Did anyone hear the phone ring?

Next thing they knew, their mom was on her way out of the door with her purse and a stuffed laundry bag.

"Good luck," their dad told her.

"Thanks," she replied as she left her family to their own devices and explanations.

On Lee Street, after the dishes were cleared, Ella stepped into her bedroom and came out with a little satchel.

"Where you going, Mama?" one of the girls asked.

"Mama's going to the hospital," Ella said. "I'm sick."

Sick? The children's eyes grew wide. She'd been up since daybreak, fixed a huge meal, helped everyone get ready for church, and sang especially well in the choir that morning. True, she had just minced at her food, but she had helped clean up the kitchen. Sick?

In a few minutes, Mrs. Mac's black Lincoln showed up at the front yard.

What's going on? the daughters wondered, looking back and forth from the car outside with its motor running to their parents as they hugged good-bye. Daddy was as quiet as ever, and Mama had a grim look on her face as she kissed each of them and carried her suitcase out to Mrs. Mac's waiting car.

"She'll be all right," Nelse promised. Then he went out back and smoked a cigarette.

Jewell pulled the Lincoln right into the ambulance bay of Forrest General Hospital, got out, and stormed through the double glass doors into the emergency waiting room.

"My employee is very ill!" she shouted. "Somebody needs to get out here and help us."

A couple of orderlies hustled out to the car with a wheelchair. Sure enough, there was a woman leaning out of the passenger side of the car, throwing up onto the asphalt.

The two men paused midstride. She was black. This wasn't the "colored" entrance.

"Hurry up!" the white woman barked directly behind their heads. "She needs help!"

So, rules be damned, the two loaded the gagging, retching Ella into the wheelchair and sped her through to the Forrest General Hospital emergency room.

She was admitted by the elegant doctor with the New Orleans accent who just happened to be in the emergency room at the time.

Jewell scatted out to the car to move it and came back with a loaded-down white laundry bag and a little satchel.

She got to the room in the "colored" area of the hospital and found a black woman attendant wiping the patient's head with a cold cloth. Only white women could be trained as nurses and nurses' aides in Mississippi. Occasionally, a black woman from another part of the country would show up with credentials, but mostly the black women who worked with patients in Mississippi hospitals had only on-the-job training.

As for her own staff at the nursing home, Jewell made sure that everyone attending to her patients had equal training, certificate award or not.

"You can leave now. I'll stay here and take care of her," Jewell told the woman, and she settled in with a book and a cup of coffee. By now, Ella was sleeping it off.

As the evening drew on, Ella was done with the stomach troubles, and Jewell shushed away anyone who tried to check on her. They spent the hours before bedtime talking about their children and wondering aloud if they could get away with this little scheme.

Jewell eventually went down to the nurse's desk, asking for a pillow and a blanket for herself. *At least there's a little cot I can sleep on,* she thought. She would not leave Ella's side until the danger had passed.

A lot of clucking and head shaking went on down at the nurse's desk. A white woman sleeping on a cot in a black patient's room was unheard of. Both Jewell and Ella were determined to break down whatever barriers they could surmount. Hospital rules were now in target.

Ella ate a good hospital breakfast. Jewell had a donut and a cup of coffee. She'd checked on the hot-water availability in the room's sink and found it somewhat lacking, but she'd do her best with it, she decided.

Bryce and Nelse paid a visit with Bryce reporting that a call had come in from the Noxubee district attorney's office. They were checking to make sure that Ella was actually in the hospital as Jesse had reported. The men suspected that someone would check on Ella's condition this morning.

"Oh, well, here we go," Ella and Jewell told each other. It was showtime.

Jewell started filling the red bladders with water as hot as possible from the room faucet. She slipped them one by one under the sheet and up next to Ella's chest and arms. For a little while, she kept one on the patient's head.

Offers of inquiry from the nurses' desk were answered with, "We're fine. No need to come in. Thanks. We'll call you if we need you."

Then the potion.

About the time Jewell was finally buzzing for a nurse, three hard knocks on the door preceded the entrance of her friend from the Forrest County district attorney's office. He was just in time to witness Ella retching into a white enamel hospital pan.

Back at his office, the assistant DA reported to his counterparts in Macon that Ella was indeed in the hospital and as sick as a dog.

Court was now scheduled for the following Monday, he reported back to Jewell.

"We'll be ready," she said.

Helpers

By Tuesday morning, Jewell was back at the convalescent center, and Ella was cooking breakfast for her group and the neighborhood.

Other than Ella's looking a little more frail than usual and Jewell's looking a little more stern, neither woman bore evidence of her Forrest General Hospital adventure the day before.

The week rocked on. Ella and Jewell waited patiently for their next trip to the hospital.

The women had learned a couple of lessons during their maiden run. First, the water wasn't hot enough in the hospital room. Second, while the vomiting and elevated temperatures were hard to question, Ella needed to at least behave as though she were sick the entire time they were in the hospital.

Jewell called her friend, the doctor.

As before, the weekend proceeded normally in both households until Sunday afternoon, when the Gaston and McMahan children were startled to learn that Ella was sick again and Jewell was transporting her to the hospital. Once again, the dads spent a lot of time in their respective backyards smoking cigarettes.

This Sunday, the admitting process was somewhat less dramatic. The kindly and refined general practitioner was once again "dropping by" when the two women arrived. The sick one was admitted; her companion proceeded to boss around the floor staff.

Bryce called Jesse as soon as he got the nod that all was in place at Forrest General Hospital.

On Monday morning, Jewell's friend from the DA's office called her at the hospital. This time, visitors from Noxubee were making a trip to the Hub City to see the situation for themselves. They were not very happy.

Soon, a parade materialized in the halls of Forrest General Hospital. It featured young men carrying suitcases into and out of Ella's room. They mostly wore Hattiesburg Convalescent Center uniforms. If this appeared unusual to the hospital staff, nobody questioned the lady in the sparkly cat-eye glasses.

By the time Jewell heard men's voices muttering down the hall and the sound of hard leather soles, Ella was in the full throes of regurgitation. Her friend stood kindly by, holding the dishpan under Ella's chin and wiping her forehead with a very warm, wet cloth.

The door swung open.

On cue, Jewell yelled into the intercom above the bed, "Nurse! Nurse! Come quick! Help! She is so sick! I don't know what to do."

Three visitors backed over one another and out of the room. The skinny one in a uniform looked like his face had caught fire.

A white nurse and a black attendant swept past them toward the patient.

"Here!" Jewell produced a thermometer. "Take her temperature! She's burning up!"

The nurse took the instrument.

"No!" Jewell directed. "She's throwing up. You'll have to take it under her arm."

The nurse dug through a mound of blankets to comply while the visitors milled around outside in the hall, grumbling and jingling.

"It's one hundred and one!" Jewell strategically aimed her voice at the door. "Call the doctor!"

That was it. The men headed for the exit, but not before the one in uniform stuck his head just inside the frame of the open door.

"See you in court," he said.

"You know we already settled that," Jewell replied and turned back to her patient.

Court was rescheduled for the following Monday.

Jewell called the doctor; this time, he balked.

"You're going to get me arrested," he said. "I just can't do this again. People were talking last weekend, and if we try this again, they'll surely know something's up," he said. "I just can't risk it."

She couldn't be mad at him, Jewell reasoned. He'd gone overboard already to help. She pondered the situation for a while.

Jewell called Ella. "We're going to have to go it alone this time," she told her friend. "Doc says he can't risk it again. We'll be okay. Just be ready about six on Sunday."

Ella replaced the receiver. "Third time's the charm," she said to the kitchen. "We can do this."

This time, Jewell and Ella announced Ella's illness after the adults had a chance to catch their Sunday afternoon naps. The women needed all the rest they could get.

It was dark by the time Jewell arrived on Lee Street to the strains of the Wonderful World of Disney's opening serenade on the Gaston's bedroom television set.

Ella kissed the children and Nelse and trundled out with her satchel in hand. Sick again.

The women both resolved to blow their way through it this time, but they recognized that the subterfuge was wearing thin. Jewell straightened her back, took a deep breath, and got out of the car at the familiar emergency room entrance. Ella was nearly to the throwing-up stage as her driver bounded through the glass doors for help. Coming in at night had ensured a different shift of workers would be there to greet her, Jewell knew.

Reworking the usual plan included a new component. Jewell had decided to enlist the baby of her family in the effort. She'd tell him all about it one day, but right now, she just needed cooperation. He loved adventure. This would be the biggest adventure of all.

Bryce notified their exasperated defense attorney.

Crossing the Road

It was one of those warm Mississippi February days as eight-year-old Mike and his buddies Carey, Phillip, and Joe Wiley hustled home from Woodley Elementary School with the sharp anticipation of at least two more hours of daylight.

This afternoon, the boys were planning a basketball game. Mike's dad had put a goal out in the backyard, and his mom chose to overlook the hard-packed, bare "court" that had unfolded beneath it. At any moment, a pick-up game could break out in the McMahan backyard. Mike wasn't the tallest player on the street, or even competitive for that matter, but he sure loved the game. His older brothers, Lynn and Gary, were at real basketball practice.

All of the neighborhood houses were on the west side of the street and looked across the way at overgrown vacant spaces. The empty lots harbored many hiding places and interesting animals every once in a while, including snakes, which everybody else's mothers were deathly afraid of. Mike's mother, on the other hand, just told him to watch where he stepped and not to bother things that didn't bother him. Snakes had just as much a right to be there as he did, she said.

Just over Mike's backyard fence was the very busy and extremely off-limits US Highway 49, alive with traffic running from the Coast through to the Delta and even more interesting, unknown points north. Across the highway sat Forrest General Hospital, where ambulances arrived at all hours of the night and day, lights and sirens blaring, and where many interesting people came and went. Mike would sometimes watch their comings and goings through his binoculars while he was out on important missions looking for Communists.

Today, there were no cars in the McMahan carport. His dad was at work, and he figured his mom was with Ella since she had gotten sick yesterday–again.

Mike expected some biscuits and syrup, or a hot sweet potato, or maybe even a piece of pie for his after-school snack waiting for him. He hurried into the kitchen. The ladies who helped his family were all good cooks, and they all knew that Mike loved to eat. Queen Esther (Esta) Harris took special pleasure in fixing Mike's favorites. Ella baked him apple pies when she was there. Occasionally, J. C. Fairley's wife, Mamie, another kindhearted cook, would manage the kitchen.

It was Esta today. She was in the kitchen all right, but what she was cooking on the stovetop wasn't food, and she hardly looked his way when he came in with his cheery "Hey, Esta." In fact, Esta stood sweating over a stack of four or five red, rubber bladders sitting by the sink. He'd seen those things before at his mom's nursing home. With a big soup ladle, Esta was dipping boiling water out of his dad's giant gumbo pot and into the skinny neck of one of the bags.

"You going to the Forrest General Hospital with these," Esta said, not taking her eyes away from her task. "Your mama said for you to get over there as quick as you got home."

Mike didn't move a muscle. He felt the blood rush to his head and heard his heart pounding away behind his ears.

"Do you hear me?" Esta asked, her voice strangely high-pitched.

"Yes, ma'am," he said. "But–"

"No buts. We ain't got time for no buts," Esta snapped. "Ella's in the hospital. Go put that stuff up and get your little traveling suitcase. I've just about got all these bags ready. Go."

Mike turned and dashed down the hall toward his bedroom, the adrenaline rush of emergency taking hold of his eight-year-old body. To begin with, Esta never talked to him or anybody else like that. Second, his mama would whip him good for going across Highway 49, and even though Esta said she wanted him to, it was a hard thing to believe.

Third, Ella must be really, really sick this time, and he loved Ella Gaston a lot. "Oh, Lord, please don't let Ella die," he whispered to himself. It was something that had worried him a lot lately. Ella was in the hospital all the time now, it seemed.

His traveling suitcase waited in its proper place on his closet floor. Mike used it when the family went to the beach or to see his grandmother in Kentucky. It had a few baseball cards and secret stuff he'd put in there for safekeeping. He dumped the treasures on the bed and took off back down the hall, the suitcase's brown plastic handle cold in his hand.

"You best tell those boys outside you ain't playing today," Esta directed, taking the suitcase from his hand.

Mike stuck his head out of the carport door and told Carey and Phillip the game was off. Nobody else could play in the backyard today either, he said. Then, "Ella's sick!" he shouted. "I'm gonna take some stuff to her at the hospital!" He couldn't resist the little boast, and Mike was smiling a little to himself when Esta rushed him.

"Don't you tell another soul about this," Esta commanded with a wagging finger.

"Yes, ma'am." Esta was so mad, it seemed.

"Here. Take this and you go out back between the fences. You look both ways before you cross that highway. I mean it. Your mama will be inside there waiting on you, and I'll be watching you. Hurry! These things are gonna get cold."

She handed him the lead-heavy suitcase. Mike feared the plastic handle wouldn't hold. After a few steps into the yard, he grabbed the handle with both hands, switching the suitcase from one side to the other every few steps to ease the weight of the thing.

Squeezing his way through the slight gap between his backyard fence and Mr. McCall's next door, Mike began his maiden trek into the forbidden territory of ditch bushes and briars, heading straight uphill to the very edge of the busy highway.

Mike set the suitcase down on the gravelly shoulder just for a minute while he stood and surveyed the route before him. The hospital looked very far away, behind the blur of steadily swishing cars.

Waiting for a lull in the traffic, Mike wiped his palms on his blue jean legs, picked up the suitcase with both hands, and stepped out onto Highway 49.

Closing Act

Jewell met little Mike at the door of Ella's room and took his suitcase. He craned his neck to see Ella. She raised a hand to greet him.

"Wait out in the hall," his mom instructed. "You can come in here in a minute." Shortly, Jewell motioned her youngest son into Ella's room. He stood quietly by the bed and patted Ella's hand.

"Ella's gonna be all right, honey baby," she assured him. "Gonna be all right. Thank you for helping me."

It was beginning to get dusk dark. Jewell told Mike he needed to get on home and take care of his homework. She'd see to Ella. He was a sad sight walking past the nurses' station as his little bowed head passed right under the sign that said "No one under fourteen allowed."

He passed a group of men in uniform headed the opposite way down the hall, and then he heard his mama's voice say, "Help! We need help in here! Ella is so sick. She is burning up with fever! Someone come here quick!"

As before, the men backed into the wall across the hall, a nurse and attendant scurried past, Jewell barked orders, Ella puked, and her fever raged.

The Old Hen Is Dead

After being reversed on appeal, preparing for trial, and calling juries three times only to be told the defendant was "sick as a dog," it was time to make a decision. Although they couldn't prove it, the prosecution up in Noxubee knew they were being played for fools. The whole fiasco needed to be done—over.

"Uncle," they said, and they asked Jesse for a way out.

They all decided the best thing to do would be to let Ella plead *nolo contendre,* or no contest, to the charge of interfering with a police officer and pay a fine. She wouldn't have a guilty plea on her record. Jesse could even handle it without her or her infernal friends in the courtroom.

Jewell got a call from her friend at the district attorney's office.

"The old hen is dead," the caller reported.

"What does that mean?" Jewell demanded.

"Just what I said. The old hen is dead, and she's not coming back."

The line went silent. It took Jewell a minute or two for the news to sink in. She headed to the Lincoln and turned it toward Lee Street.

On February 25, a plea of *nolo contendre* was entered into the court record for Circuit Court Case No. 3644 in Noxubee County. Defendant Gaston was ordered to pay $250 and court costs. District Attorney Buck entered a motion of *nole pross* on Ella's carrying a concealed weapon charge, and it went to the file.

Just like Jewell had predicted, Ella Gaston never went back to jail, and she never set foot back in that courtroom.

It was all over—except for the secret-keeping.

EPILOGUE

The Gastons

That Ella was a changed person after the "incident" was acknowledged by those who knew her well. She was a little more reflective, a little quieter, and a whole lot more determined to offer her quiet, special gifts to those she cared about, including the gift of keeping secrets for a lifetime.

During the summer of 2011, her daughters—Jean, then of Boston, and Voncile, then of Los Angeles—returned home to Hattiesburg for the annual Newman Quarters reunion. They and hundreds of their former neighbors and classmates center their summer travel excursions around the yearly gatherings, which occur on or around July 4. On this particular day, they were pleased when the preacher spoke lovingly from the pulpit about their mother and the influence she had on him and their contemporaries.

It was also there they met someone again who had disappeared from their lives in 1964, someone whom Voncile didn't want to name in print—even after all these years—due to the "danger to his family." He was their brother Clifford's best friend in high school. Like so many of their generation, this young man had gotten involved in the Freedom Summer activities that invaded Hattiesburg with hope and an idea of first-class citizenship for the black residents of the various quarters around the Hub City.

What he did to run afoul of the law, they never learned, but it was remarkable enough to cause him to flee the state. He had remained away for years, the girls found out at the reunion.

What he told them about their mother, though, was a stunner. Ella had acted as an intermediary between the refugee and his family, her neighbors. He called her weekly, disguising his voice in case recorders were going. They spoke in code, and Ella would make the trip down the street to report his safety to his frantic family.

One night, she had to tell him the sad news of his grandmother's passing, their friend told the daughters. When he started to cry on the phone, Ella comforted him. "Be a man, now. You're a man, now. Don't cry. It will be all right. Don't cry."

He would never forget her kindness to him, he said nearly fifty years later. She was a quiet angel.

Although the sisters were once again learning for the first time that their mother had been secretly engaged in something so important, they weren't really surprised. The Gaston children had grown up as community caregivers.

Their dad, the dapper Nelse, had built a little barber shop in the family backyard where he'd offer the latest haircut styles to the neighborhood men and boys. A number of the men at the 2011 reunion were former clients.

Many of them also recalled the days when a Friday night meant that the Lee Street world would gather on the Gastons' front porch or in their living room listening to Nelse's strong radio as Floyd Patterson showed out in the boxing ring. The "Look Sharp/Be Sharp" march that opened the *Gillette Cavalcade of Sports* was a fitting anthem for an event orchestrated by the good-looking Nelse Gaston.

Ella continued throughout her life in her quest to feed the hungry. In a neighborhood of mixed economic abilities, there were families who had less wherewithal than the Gastons. These families would receive tender offerings from Ella's kitchen. The children were continually sent scurrying to one house or the other with food. One evening, Jean was dispatched with a large container of fresh chicken broth to the home of an elderly neighbor who was very ill and refusing food. Ella was especially worried about him. Cupping a bowl of the warm comfort in her lap, Jean sat by the man's bedside and spoon-fed him the entire contents. He thanked her gently and leaned back on his pillow. The next morning, the Gastons learned he'd died in his sleep. Ella and Jean had provided perhaps his last glimpse of human kindness.

A young man of the neighborhood who was a deaf-mute took up with the Gastons and spent a lot of his time in their home, quietly participating in the boisterous goings-on inside the neighborhood gathering spot. Eventually, he went off to the deaf school in Jackson. On his trips home, he taught his adopted family how to sign so they could communicate with him and he could tell them about his life. When he graduated, the entire Gaston family loaded up and made the hour-and-a-half trek up Highway 49 for the ceremony. And they were all in attendance at his wedding a few years later.

Nelse continued working for the Pine Burr Meat Packing Company, even when it became a subsidiary of the Merchant Company. He eventually went to work for Marshall Durbin in one of their chicken processing plants. Long before, he'd built an extra bedroom and bath on the back of the house where he'd go clean up after work. Ella didn't cotton to smelly work clothes around her living and cooking environments.

Occasionally, Nelse would join his friends for a night on the town. One evening, a group of the guys were enjoying life at the Do Drop Inn in the Tatum Woods Quarters when a fight broke out in the parking lot. Someone with a knife was slashing into a guy they all knew as Red. No one was moving to defend him, though they all surely knew that if the attack continued, Red would die before their eyes. Nelse shouted at the assailant to stop, but the knife-wielder never slowed up. Unwilling to watch a murder, Nelse wrapped his jacket around his arm and waded into the fight. Bludgeoning the attacker with his wrapped arm, Nelse was able to wrest the knife from him. That night, Nelse showed up at home covered in blood. The children cried and cried, thinking he had been shot or cut. No, he said, he'd just helped a friend. Red didn't die, but he spent weeks in the hospital hovering on the edge of a grave.

One of Ella's great goals in life was to see her children educated, and they did not disappoint their mama. Jean earned her bachelor of science degree in health and human services from Springfield College, Boston; Clifford attended Northeast University; Juanita received a business degree from the Mildred Louise School of Business in East St. Louis; Leauvelle received a degree from the Los Angeles Trade Technical College and worked as an engineer for Lockheed Aircrafts; Michael attended the University of Massachusetts; Hermene earned college credits; and Voncile received her undergraduate degrees in business education and psychology from William Carey College and a master's degree in school counseling and psychology from California State University at Los Angeles.

There is nothing left now of the embracing Lee Street community except the ruffle-edged pavement of abandoned streets, a stoic magnolia tree, familiar pines and mimosas, and a few fruit trees. Everything else is bush-hogged grass. The land sits quietly shimmering in the way living things do when their sunlight is filtered through the breath of a nearby body of water.

After the Gaston children were mostly grown and gone, the Leaf River overran its banks one too many times, flooding the neat wooden homes again, drowning already salvaged pictures and trophies, curling the linoleum and gobbing up the furniture. Yes, it was one time too many.

The City of Hattiesburg, under the leadership of Mayor Bobby Chain, purchased the properties of the Gastons and their neighbors, and all the residents dispersed, carrying with them nothing much except the warm and wonderful memories of their own little sanctuary out by the river in the Newman Quarters.

Nelse passed away of prostate cancer in 1994, and Ella began the long journey of life as a widow. As her own health began to fail, she moved to Voncile's in Los Angeles after a lengthy stay at Jean's in Boston. Ella succumbed to the aftermath of a stroke on February 21, 2005, a day shy of the forty-sixth anniversary of "the incident."

The McMahans

"You might think Mom's house is over the top inside," Mike warned me during our pre-interview meeting at Shoney's on Highway 49 in September 2010. "She believes in decorating everything up. And that was the same way she decorated her nursing home. People couldn't believe it was a nursing home the way she had it done. Everything had to be just so."

At his mother's establishment, patients dined on gourmet food while seated on gold ballroom chairs, surrounded by generous flower arrangements and lavish draperies. Its central lobby and public areas were tastefully decorated in grand style, and closely tended grounds teemed with color. Residents' rooms were "nicely done," as Jewell liked to describe décor suiting her standards.

For fifty-five years, Jewell was the owner and operator of the Hattiesburg Convalescent Center on Bay Street until her retirement party in 2009, an event that brought in about 250 people to pay their respects to her and entailed the City of Hattiesburg providing a trolley to transport guests back and forth to their parking places.

At one point, eighteen Hattiesburg doctors had their mothers registered in the Hattiesburg Convalescent Center as clients, Mike said. He related the story of running into a colleague whose specialty was suing nursing homes for negligence. He told Mike that if his office ever received a call about the Hattiesburg Convalescent Center, his staff was under threat if they accepted the case. No matter how many times they'd looked through the convalescent center's files for wrongdoing, there was none to be found. It was an expensive and losing cause, the lawyer surmised, and so he wasn't interested in wasting his time and money on it. Mike, himself a trial lawyer, counted that conversation as a testimony to the fine service his mother's staff gave to their residents.

Jewell drew on her business school teaching and worked with female employees to make sure they were equipped to survive and prevail in the world. Jewell held etiquette classes in which she taught the women how to walk into a room with their shoulders back and their heads up, how to talk directly to people and shake hands, not slump, and not chomp on gum.

Commendations, newspaper articles, certificates, profiles, and plaques of appreciation for Jewell in recognition of her outstanding lifelong achievements in the nursing home industry and as a contributing citizen of her accidental hometown lined a long hallway in her home.

Jewell once called colorfully to task the great Alton B. Cobb, MD, who steered Mississippi's State Department of Health for many years. Mike, the lawyer son, had memorized the scene as a stunned eyewitness.

This was after a committee refused to grant a certificate of need for her son Lynn's eye surgery center in 1980. It was an innovative idea—patients would have surgery in a facility other than a hospital. They'd be given pre- and postsurgical care comparable to that of a hospital, complete with nurses, doctors, and recovery rooms. Patients would go home the same day as their procedures. Nothing like it had ever been tried in Mississippi.

Mississippi state law requires hospitals to be granted a "certificate of need," or CON, by the health department before being allowed to open a facility. What seems a straightforward enough request to do business often turns into a nasty fight between service providers, one trying to protect its turf and the other trying to gain yardage.

This time, the battle was between provider and regulatory agency.

At the announcement denying her son's request, Jewell stood.

"Do you agree a surgical center such as this would save taxpayer money?" she queried as well as any lawyer's daughter, which she was.

"Yes" was the answer.

"Do you agree this surgical center would provide better safety for patients?"

"Yes, ma'am."

"Do you agree this surgical center would make care more affordable for patients?"

"Yes, it would."

"Well then ..." she said, and then she told them all exactly what she thought of them.

The hearing room fell dead silent. Dr. Cobb suggested a brief meeting of the committee in executive session. They retired to a back room. After a few minutes, the committee resumed their seats.

"The committee has met and decided to grant the certificate of need to the Southern Eye Center."

Jewell picked up her purse and exited the meeting room, followed by a team of stunned New York lawyers and her unsurprised sons.

"You know, people thought we really had money," Mike said. "But in truth, my daddy just liked to give. When he died, we were just about broke. But Daddy always said, 'Community service is rent we pay to live in a good community.'"

At her 2012 birthday bash, Jewell confirmed that she and Bryce had made a covenant to give away a quarter of their income.

Bryce was big and strong with hands like hams, Mike said.

"If you ran your car off in a ditch, he was the kind of guy who could literally pick it up and move it out, " Mike said. "He would take fifty-pound bags of feed, one in each hand, and toss them into the back of a truck like he was throwing a newspaper.

"Back in the sixties, when they were raising money for a big building project at Temple Baptist church, Dad came up with an idea to sell bonds to congregation members as a way to finance the building. He sold all the bonds and promised investors they would actually make money on the deal," Mike said. "The next year, Dad went around and convinced all the investors to donate their bond proceeds back to the church. That's the kind of guy he was."

In keeping with the family philanthropic mandate, ophthalmologist son Lynn went on to win awards for giving. His website said, "Dr. McMahan established Southern Eye Center's Gift of Sight Program, in which free surgery is provided for needy patients. The program won *USA Today*'s National Make a Difference Award and was featured in *USA Weekend* magazine. Dr. McMahan is also one of only four ophthalmologists honored as a Person of Vision by the Mississippi Foundation to Preserve Sight."

Of her three sons, the one who looked the most like their dad was Gary, who had died at age sixty only a few months before I met his mother. He was her administrative helper at the Convalescent Center for thirty-five years and, true to the family's adventurous leanings, an avid skydiver. On the day we met, Jewell was still not used to the idea of his being gone, but length of life had taught her that it must go on. And so she was going on.

Bryce McMahan, once the mighty, undisputed heavyweight champion of Mississippi; Perkinston Junior College football star; real estate developer; stalwart board of education president; and happy giver, died from a ruptured blood vessel in August 1971. His chest wall had been weakened and burned from intense cobalt cancer treatments, and a major artery exploded one morning as he bent over to tie his shoes. With him was Willie Ruth Twilley Jones, who, as a little girl, had watched TV at Miz Ella's, and who had been a longtime employee and friend to the McMahans. Mike had just come in from life as a USM freshman for a home-cooked lunch to find Willie Ruth lifting his bleeding father into the front seat of the family car.

Mike jumped into the driver's seat just as Jewell swung into the driveway. She crawled across the back seat to cradle her husband's head from behind during the dreadful ride. He bled out on the way to the hospital.

"They told me he was dead at the hospital, but I didn't believe it," Jewell said. "I had his blood all over me, but it just couldn't be. I knew, you know. But I still wouldn't believe it."

She never remarried because she couldn't find anyone else who measured up to Bryce McMahan, she said. "He was the love of my life."

After Bryce died, Jewell realized that without a massive cash infusion into her nursing home business, she would not be able to carry on as they'd planned. She approached the men of First Federal Bank in Hattiesburg for a $750,000 loan. The McMahans had always enjoyed the trust of the officers of First Federal. Jewell and Bryce had financed McMahan real estate developments, businesses, homes, and everything else through this bank. So, naturally, when the cash crunch came, Jewell did what she and Bryce had always done. She went to the bank, but this time she was alone.

"So Mom gets called into her banker's office the next day," Mike related. "They've all met, and because she is a woman, you know, they don't want to give her the loan by herself. So he says, 'Jewell, we'll give you this loan, but your three sons have to sign onto the note.'"

"Oh, really," she said. "We'll see about that."

None of the sons was listed on any of their parents' properties. *Outrageous*, she decided.

The next day, Jewell asked for a meeting with Zeke Powell, the unfortunate banker who had delivered the news. In she walked with a document she placed on his desk. It had blue paper on the back. She looked him straight in the eye. "You know what this is?" she asked him. "This is a *federal* lawsuit against you and this bank on grounds of discrimination against me because I am a woman. And you know what else? When I win this lawsuit, which I will, I'll own this bank and you'll be out of a job—you and everybody else here."

With that, she strode out of the office.

Everybody in Mississippi who paid any attention at all to national news had heard of discrimination lawsuits by then. The papers on Mr. Powell's desk portended a change in how the bank would conduct its business with female clients from here on out. He called a little confab with his bank officers.

The next day, Jewell McMahan signed the loan papers and, from that day forward, never did banking business with any banker other than Zeke Powell.

Mr. Powell was an honored guest at Jewell's gala retirement party, as was Dr. Cobb.

The Farrars

After a term as sheriff, Marian Farrar demurred and allowed Emmett to regain his standing as chief law enforcement officer of Noxubee County in 1963.

When the Sovereignty Commission was making one of its many "investigatory" rounds during the 1960s, in an effort to quiet the "northern press," it inquired of sheriffs statewide to report how many black officers they employed. Farrar's scrawling hand can be seen on the Noxubee reply form—"Not a damn one—let the Northern Press go to hell & mind their business. Emmett W. Farrar, Sheriff."

It was speculated that by 1967, enough blacks in Noxubee County were registered to vote to use their bloc to defeat Farrar despite his reported continued struggle to undermine any potential black organizational efforts.

His last year in office, 1967, was the year that Farrar was indicted by a federal grand jury for intimidating black Noxubee parents who had enrolled their children in the all-white schools. Most of them withdrew their children's registrations.

Following is what the court case records say was Sheriff Farrar's participation in the efforts to quell school choice for black parents.

> Appellee Emmett W. Farrar, Sheriff of Noxubee County, was present at the courthouse when Mastrow Oliver delivered the choice forms of a number of Negro parents who had chosen to send their children to white schools. According to Oliver, he was met by a crowd of 15-18 men, including Farrar, standing in a hallway when he delivered the forms, and Sheriff Farrar stated that 'you ain't got no damn sense,' that he would 'break' Oliver's

neck and that he wanted to talk to Oliver after he had finished in the School Superintendent's office. Oliver also testified that Sheriff Farrar served him with a summons on one of the debt collection suits that had been filed against him, and that Farrar had said at that time that Oliver would be getting more and more suits filed against him because 'you niggers were going to stir up something anyhow.' Farrar also allegedly said that he would no longer protect Oliver. Appellee Farrar denied making these statements. However, he admitted that he was present when Nelson Short withdrew his choice of a white school and that he told Short 'I thought he was doing the best thing for his children.' Farrar also was present when appellee Lanier brought Mrs. Beck and Mrs. Jackson to the Superintendent of Education's office to change their choices, and he witnessed the papers for the withdrawal of a choice by one Oscar Ivey.

Despite the threats, though, there was one black student who stayed enrolled at Shuqualak High School and received his diploma–Franklin Eugene Hill, Frank Ed Hill's nephew and namesake.

The Farrars' two children each became successful educators. Emmett Jr. was a petroleum engineer working as an instructor of automation and control technology at East Mississippi Community College's Mayhew Campus when he died in 2004 at age sixty-one. Their daughter, Linda, taught in the public schools and was hired for her first teaching position by Superintendent of Education Reecy Dickson, Noxubee's first black elected official. Linda was on faculty under Velma Hill Jenkins, the school principal and sister of Frank Ed.

As for Mrs. Farrar, she was portrayed by those I spoke with as a kind and friendly person but one who, like her husband, never quite understood why her husband's deeds were so controversial.

Emmett Farrar died of cancer in the mid-seventies and is buried at the Salem Methodist Church Cemetery close by the school and homestead of his childhood. Mrs. Farrar still lived in Noxubee County at the time of this writing.

AUTHOR'S NOTES

A few things need explaining in greater detail than is possible in a prologue with its intrinsic need to set tone and atmosphere, introduce a plotline and main characters, and not put the reader to sleep before the story opens. And so, I compiled these notes.

For instance, it may seem incredible to some that this story was kept a secret for so long from so many people. First, the threat of retribution and arrest was a very real concern for Jewell McMahan. She was terrified of being arrested, even decades after these events, and so waited fifty years to tell the story. Now having delved into the realities of the times involved, I understand her fear. As late as 2012, it was the same fear that kept Ella's daughters from revealing the name of their childhood friend who had fled Newman Quarters so long ago.

Second, the McMahan family agreed to not discuss this occurrence outside of the group of people who already knew about it—themselves and the few other individuals involved. They knew that Ella and Nelse did not want their children to know about their jail time or the humiliation of the trial, even though the little ones had witnessed "the incident." Voncile, Jean, and Mike all attested to this as truth.

Jewell, at this writing, is still a very vibrant, engaged woman. I am fortunate to have captured her recollections on tape. Those taped interviews form the basis of the narrative.

I marveled at the detail in Jewell's memory of events that happened as many as seventy years prior. I knew that everyone involved was a product of the times, and that their actions—even though courageous—may not be viewed as entirely up to modern standards in matters of race relations. Nevertheless, I determined to tell the story as true to the circumstances, culture, and mores of the times as possible.

And I knew that the telling would by needs include some plot point vignettes that were not necessarily documented but, nevertheless completely plausible for the times and characters.

I shared the manuscript with some individuals during the book-writing period. On December 5, 2012, at his mother's ninety-fourth birthday celebration at the Hattiesburg Depot, Mike was allowed to tell the story to a group of about sixty partygoers. The buzz about *Justice for Ella* started that night.

Facing the dilemma of how to portray the racial labels of the times, I determined to capitalize *Negro* and incorporate the terms *nigger* and *colored* into the narrative where they were either actually used or most likely used, though the terms are personally abhorrent to me and to most sensible individuals of the twenty-first century.

When trying to decide how best to tell the tale of *Justice for Ella*, I determined it was important to make every effort to develop the major characters, most of whom played out their lives very far off the public stage. I relied on interviews with people who knew them, experienced them, heard them speak, and observed them in various walks of life.

Additionally, I made efforts to set their narrative against the defining moments of the age in which it is set. As with any nonfiction-based story, many more details of the characters and period would have made for very interesting reading, but, alas, they only served to bog down the narrative. It was painful to let them go.

Ella's daughters, though they witnessed their parents' arrests, were unaware of the lengthy aftermath resulting from that afternoon. It is difficult in this technologically infused era for us to realize that some matters were really kept secret in the past. Apparently, Ella and Nelse were most adept at the practice. The Gaston daughters provided the details of the day, even down to what their mother and father were wearing, the travel food, and the travel games the family played.

The chapter "Driving While Black" opens the book with a version of the incident that sparked the story. The term "driving while black" is a vernacular version of "driving while drunk" that is commonly used to denote that a black person behind the wheel is often pulled over for interrogation simply because of the color of his or her skin. This version was gleaned from Jewell McMahan's retelling of Ella's report to her. Subsequent discussions with Ella's daughters, Jean and Voncile, affirmed most of what Jewell had related, and their recollections form the point of view for the more detailed narrative of the event, which unfolds in the chapter entitled "Up Home." There are subtle differences in the versions, which is typical of eyewitness accounts and their retelling by third parties.

In keeping with the effort to round out the characters, I divided the text into background sections for both Ella and Jewell, which also tangentially revealed their families. I followed those sections with the "Up Home" retelling and background of the incident and the legal wrangling that followed it, culminating in the successful scheme concocted to make sure the ultimate goal was achieved–Ella never went back to jail.

It should be noted that during the time, and even in some quarters today, the term *Civil War* is avoided in the South. Euphemisms in defense of the South's rebellion, such as "the War Between the States," "the War for Southern Independence," or "the Lost Cause" are favored by some to this very day. These designations are used here to emphasize the overarching remnants of plantation mentality that prevailed well into the twentieth century in Mississippi.

"The Southern Way of Life" is a euphemism that was used repeatedly during Mississippi's white supremacy days as a more genteel way of saying "segregated society," or at least some people believed it was. Today, it has morphed into "Our Way of Life." I dare say most African Americans recognize it for what it is, especially when it appears in political materials.

Noxubee County, I discovered, bears a very rich history of political prominence in Mississippi's strict segregationist era, beginning with the incursion of white planters who introduced African slaves into the population. The chapter "Noxubee" was developed from numerous historical documents, which revealed details of county history that I believe informed the circumstances protecting racism in the area for at least a century after the Civil War, well into the time of the incident involving the Gastons.

The chapter concerning Dorroh Hill Road offers a description of the community in which Ella and Nelse were raised. I was able to characterize its vibrancy through an interview with Ella's cousin John Lewis, a current Dorroh Hill Road resident, as well as an interview with State Representative Reecy Dickson (D-Macon) who described her own insulated upbringing as typical of the way in which many black people lived their lives by necessity in Noxubee County during the twentieth century. Historical documents provided the pedigrees and influence of the Dorroh-area family to the area.

The descriptions of Ella's upbringing are consistent with her daughters' recollections of Ella's stories. I interviewed Voncile and Jean at Jewell McMahan's home. Additionally, during several telephone conversations with Jean, she relayed the relationship her mother had described with her caretaker, Aunt Ella. Ella's daughters described the circumstances of their parents' marriage, and cousin John described the house where Ella lived and how it related to Nelse's childhood home.

Anyone who knew Nelse personally confirmed that he was most particular about taking care of his things, especially his vehicles. I chose to emphasize this character aspect of Nelse's because it stands as a complete contradiction to the driving behavior described by the lawmen who arrested him.

I was reassured that after reading an initial manuscript, both daughters stated that they believed the characterizations of their parents were accurate.

I pulled most of the information about the Newman Quarters (or Lee Street community) from records provided by Ella's daughters, including the statement by a neighbor about the bus incident and the activities in which the children engaged. Jean provided the narrative of how Nelse and Ella wound up in Hattiesburg and the progression of their living circumstances in the Quarters. Willie Ruth Twilley Jones was a child in the neighborhood and a contemporary of Ella's daughters. She provided information about Ella's mothering position within the community and confirmed the "playground" like atmosphere of the Gastons' yard. She also described the habits of the neighborhood mothers regarding caring for their homes and families. The daughters remembered troops of neighbors on hand for meals. Ms. Twilley Jones provided the church descriptions of Nelse, Ella, and the congregation and the reactions of the neighborhood after "the incident." Jean told the story of the tragedy involving a neighbor's grandchild, which was reported briefly in the *Hattiesburg American*.

Her children's getting an education was a paramount goal of Ella's, according to her daughters and Ms. Twilley Jones. Ella's foray into the kitchen of the Hattiesburg Convalescent Center was a result of that drive.

The daughters, her coworkers, Mike, and Mrs. Mac all provided insight into Ella's talent as a cook. If frying chicken is an art form in the South, Ella Gaston was a blue ribbon artist in the medium, I surmised, since nearly everyone I spoke to about her mentioned "Ella" and "fried chicken" in the same sentence at least once. I felt this particular talent deserved a mention.

I was struck by the reactions of every woman I interviewed who actually knew Nelse Gaston. To the person, they all smiled, nodded, and spoke of how handsome he was, and one even fanned her face. The details about Nelse's fashion choices were provided by his daughters and Ms. Twilley.

As for Ella's demeanor after the incident, Jewell described it thusly: "She was never the same. It did something to her she just couldn't overcome. She worked as she could, but never full-time again."

Jewell described her own first night in Hattiesburg in great detail, including her interaction with the black gentleman who helped her. I felt it important to introduce Forrest County with a mention of the lingering influence of its namesake, Confederate General Nathan Bedford Forrest, at the time of Jewell's arrival.

While researching the general, I stumbled into the fascinating Congressional hearings of 1871 concerning the Ku Klux Klan and there discovered the role Noxubee County played in the racial struggles of the post-Civil War era in Mississippi. Ironically, nearly one hundred years later, Noxubee County was the setting for Ella's story. Also ironically, today, every Noxubee County elected official is black.

I was treated to a tour of the beautifully restored Hattiesburg Train Depot in the fall of 2010 and was a celebrating partygoer there when Jewell observed her birthday in the grand hall in December 2012. I gained details of the depot, Hattiesburg, and the prewar era through research into newspapers, histories of Hattiesburg, and the lumber industry as well as a look into rail lore, customs, and materials provided by the station. I believed the convergence of Camp Shelby's resurgence, the textbook controversy, a legendary jail break in Arkansas, and the inflammatory campaign of Senator Theodore Bilbo created a portentous frame for Jewell's first night in Mississippi.

Remarkably, Forrest County Agricultural High School stands today almost unchanged from that morning in 1940 when Jewell was driven onto campus by her irritated headmaster. Current school secretary Linda Ainsworth provided confirmation of Jewell's employment dates at the institution. The small town of Brooklyn remains, but in reduced circumstances, like so many of its sister towns across Mississippi. I found its interesting naming history in WPA writings and paid a visit there with a friend one summer afternoon in 2011 to inquire about the history of its retail center. My descriptions of the town stem from that visit. It was there I learned about which stores were likely the ones Jewell encountered on that Sunday morning so long ago. I learned a gentleman named Walley was the local pharmacist. I could not make sure that Walley was the kind person who helped Jewell, so I named that character after my late cousin, Edward Walker, a beloved pharmacist from Covington County.

I felt it important to explore the Eastern Kentucky ethos and the family culture that had helped form Jewell's strong personality. In Mississippi, we are somewhat familiar with the "Appalachian Attitude" that is evident in Northeast Mississippi's foothills areas. It is not something one contradicts very successfully, no matter how nicely we try to do it in the Deep South. I came to understand that the strong-willed persona Jewell has exhibited throughout her life likely came from early total immersion in the mountain culture. Listening to the many partygoers at her 2012 birthday party tell their stories about the honoree convinced me I was right.

Interestingly, the infamous Tug Fork was the victim of one of the worst coal mining disasters in American history in 2000 when the Martin County Coal Company impoundment collapsed and sent 250 million gallons of raw coal slurry into the picturesque valley. Images of a drowned and buried Tug Fork raced around the globe as an example of the worst-case scenario becoming a reality in terms of coal spill disasters. Inez, Jewell's hometown, was ground zero for the spill. It wasn't the first time Inez was in the news.

It was from the front porch of Tommy Fletcher's rundown cabin on the outskirts of Inez that President Lyndon Johnson announced his War on Poverty in April 1964. Inez thus became the image of the third-world living conditions that plagued much of Appalachia and the Southeast and prompted Congress's passage of a number of social services acts during the sixties.

The president had come to Inez to make his announcement at the invitation of Jewell's brother, Martin County Superintendent of Education Shelton Clark. After that visit, Shelton's impoverished students who attended school hungry, weak, and thus less than able to learn, enjoyed at least one hot meal per day thanks to the federal government's free lunch program—a result of the War on Poverty their town had helped launch. Today, the Inez high school is named for the innovative school superintendent.

Jewell related the love story between Bryce and her, including the honeymoon night, much to Mike's delighted surprise. He was also stunned to hear the story of the overturned car incident. He had already told me about his dad's hands, and I surmise that Bryce had picked the car up himself. I wanted to make sure that their story was told against the youth culture of the moment and so researched headlines and trends for the era. Jewell was a dancer in her youth and even into her nineties. In 2010, she showed me the dancing shoes she'd worn on a cruise the summer before to prove it.

Mike and numerous publications provided the descriptions of Mrs. Mac's work ethic. The issue of Mississippi's typical "separate" employee accoutrements was aired out quite well in Katherine Stockett's *The Help*; but, according to her family, Jewell was a groundbreaker in bucking the segregated workplace system in Hattiesburg, and in her own home as well.

"The ladies who stayed with us were given the same authority over us as our parents. Willie Ruth [Twilley Jones] can tell my mom what to do to this day. She ruled the roost in our family for a long time," Mike told me.

I noted on the day that Mike and I sat down with Ms. Twilley Jones at her house for the interview that, as soon as Mike took his seat, she told him to go get her a glass of tea from the kitchen, which he promptly did.

Although there was only one living adult witness to the events surrounding the courtroom story that I could locate, Shuqualak and Macon remain in appearance today much as they were in 1959. An exception is that Shuqualak's downtown area was devastated by a fire, but the residential areas are mostly intact.

The interview with Nelse's nephew John Lewis as well as my visit to the home place helped provide details to fill out the chronology of the day. Voncile provided a description of the family's traditional leaving ritual, significant in its juxtaposition with the claims of the arresting officers offered in court. The number and names of the officers and their means of transportation were gleaned from the circuit court trial testimony.

I made the effort to understand the original lay of the town of Shuqualak with numerous windshield tours around town. And I took two big rocks home from the gravelly Dorroh Hill Road, after stopping by the Slaughter Family Cemetery.

Although local newspapers reported the attack on Marshal Ollice Moore that allegedly sparked the arrest of the Gastons, I was honored to interview Mayor Velma Jenkins of Shuqualak, whose brother Frank Ed Hill was the actual object of the manhunt. As she relayed the horrors of that dark Saturday night, her eyes welled with tears and emotion choked her sturdy voice. It was hard for her, even after all these years. She was quick to say that she held no sense of retribution and made every effort to treat everyone she encountered as an equal.

Frank Ed never told anyone how he was able to disappear and wind up in Centerville, Illinois, where Viola and his children joined him, and he eventually retired from U.S. Steel. Pete Flora never said if he had played any role in the escape, and no one had the nerve to ask. He was widely respected by the black people of Noxubee County as a fair and honest man, and that sentiment remained true some thirty years after his death, as best I could ascertain.

Jewell described how Jesse Stennis became involved in the case with a call from Curran Sullivan, the lawyer who rented office space above the Beard and McMahan Realty Company. I learned that Edwin L. Pittman, who gained his law license in 1960, became a partner in Curran Sullivan's law firm. Pittman eventually became attorney general, secretary of state, and then chief justice of the Mississippi State Supreme Court. Curran's son Michael, who joined his father in the practice in 1966, became a presiding Supreme Court Justice. All in all, the second floor of Beard and McMahan Realty served as an effective incubator for a remarkable pair of public servants.

Mike and I paid a visit to the old McMahan office, toured the upstairs, peered out of the front windows, and shot a picture of Bryce's favored mode of entrance–the loading dock ladder attached to the back of the building. Significantly, the building now houses the Mississippi Center for Legal Services Corporation, a nonprofit whose mission is to ensure "Equal Justice for All."

The informality of the justice of the peace system in Mississippi was quite evident in the paperwork produced for this case. The affidavit of the sheriff presented to Judge Watkins in which he described the circumstances of Ella's charge was sworn to and signed on February 24, the day of the trial. The warrant for Ella's arrest was filed on the same day. The record of proceedings shows that the sheriff arrested and jailed Ella on February 23, the day prior to the Watkins bond proceeding. Additionally, the record of proceedings shows that everything took place before T. E. Woodfin.

Charlie Watkins, son of Justice of the Peace H. H. Watkins, provided details about his father's businesses and practices as a JP as well as confirming the Bull Deale story, which I first encountered as a recorded online history by Charlie Staten. Charlie Watkins actually saw the severed head sitting on the counselor's podium in the courthouse.

Jewell provided the circumstances and dialogue surrounding her remarkably rapid trip from Hattiesburg to Shuqualak during Ella and Nelse's first bond hearing. I believe I know who the unlucky deputy in the parking lot was, but we will never know for sure. I also suspect he was the likely foil for Jewell during the circuit court trial and in the hospital. While it may seem outrageous that a Southern woman would talk to a law enforcement official like Jewell McMahan did, Mike assured me that the same language was in every telling of the story he had heard for fifty years.

My forays into Macon included research in the newspaper morgue at Chancery Clerk Mary Shelton's office; a tour of the courthouse by Circuit Clerk Carl Mickens, whose courtroom has remained virtually unchanged from the date of the trial; a look at the cited arrest docket; an interview with a courthouse custodian who described the segregated entrances and facilities; interviews with Representative Reecy Dickson and Macon mayor Bob Boykin; chats with newspaper editor Scott Boyd; a cruise by Jesse Stennis's red brick house; a look inside his little white office, thanks to Bill Liston; and research conducted within the restored jail, now a lively community library, thanks in part to the Flora family influence.

I was particularly fascinated by the jail. Built in 1907, the Romanesque structure was in service until 1977, housing prisoners and their wardens' families alike. Its architect, W. S. Hull, built such iconic structures as the Covington County courthouse and the first addition to the Mississippi Governor's Mansion. In 1982 the abandoned jail was adopted by forward-thinking preservationists led by F. S. Flora Jr., Pete's son, who envisioned it as the perfect site for the central county library, according to library materials. Today, visitors are welcomed through the former residence's front door into a fully staffed library teeming with activity. Upstairs, stuffed animals line the cell bars and GED classes are underway while children read and research on computers. The old prisoner entryway has been replaced by a modern enclosed stairway and elevator. The hangman's apparatus is still at the top of the thirteen stairs, its gallows lever held closed by a small padlock.

While the story of Alec and Bull makes for a great Southern gothic tale, legends and rumors still lurk about Sheriff Farrar's alleged heavy-handed and brutal treatment of the black citizens who came into unfortunate contact with him. He enforced the rules regarding no white shirts for black men, stepping off the sidewalk to allow white people to pass, and a myriad of other offenses "uppity" blacks could commit in the county, it is said. Those I interviewed remembered him in this way.

I made efforts to uncover some less dreadful information than what had been portrayed in the record and recollections of those aware of "the incident" or who had personal knowledge of Sheriff Farrar and his career as Noxubee County's chief law enforcement officer. A mitigating resource emerged from a most unlikely quarter. The enigmatic Ike Brown, legendary Democratic political activist from Macon, allowed the former lawman some latitude. Brown said that by the time he arrived in Noxubee County in the early 1970s, Farrar's sting had subsided. According to Brown, the tale went that after his 1967 defeat, the old sheriff was known to ask citizens if he was really as bad as people said. It seemed as though Farrar actually was unable to comprehend that his actions, which Brown believes were orchestrated by powerful white money interests, were so reprehensible to society.

"He was kind of pitiful as he got older," Brown remembered. "He just didn't get it."

In addition to my ventures into Noxubee County and recording hours of interviews with Jewell, Ella's daughters, and others who had knowledge of the case, I spent hours poring through newspaper and Sovereignty Commission files at the Mississippi Department of Archives and History and pulling research materials from verifiable sources online. A select number of these resources are noted in the bibliography.

I could never locate any justice court records about the case. Everyone I spoke with agreed that record keeping was at the discretion of the presiding judge. It wasn't until 1983 that the legislature passed laws to centralize the courts' record keeping and required every county to have a justice court clerk, functioning similarly to chancery and circuit court clerks.

Jewell explained why she and Ella were so determined that Ella wouldn't spend another day in jail and why she and Bryce were willing to expend whatever resources were necessary, including putting their home up as collateral, to make sure it didn't happen. She said, in her usual frank way, that they thought Ella "would be used as a whore if she had to spend time in jail."

Court documents and filings helped form the characterizations of the lawyers, staffers, and various witnesses in the trial and in the narrative drive. I carved out only the segments of court testimony necessary to move the plot forward and prove salient points. And I felt compelled to preserve the folksy dialogue of the litigators.

Political experiences, ambitions, and roles of the lead and supporting players were documented in the *Macon Beacon*, the *Clarion-Ledger*, the *Hattiesburg American*, and several Blue Books, Mississippi's *Official and Statistical Register*'s.

My friend John Christopher, a Columbus native, happened to be an eyewitness to the Jon Mattox murder trial and filled in the detail of Judge Greene's behavior toward Jesse during that proceeding and the fact that the judge smoked in court. John, along with Mayor Boykin, provided descriptions of Attorney Stennis's courtroom behaviors and physical appearance.

Disappointingly, while defending Jon Mattox, Jesse used a tactic sure to cast doubt on his client's guilt—he mentioned a rumor about three unfamiliar black men having been seen in the vicinity of Mrs. Tate's home on the morning of her murder. No one else testified to remembering the rumor. The tool of injecting racial prejudice into court proceedings was not yet done.

Judge Greene was still serving in 1968 when the first female jurors were allowed to be seated after State Senator Helen Muirhead of Hinds County sneaked the word *person's* as a replacement for *his* into the 1967 bill amending the juror statutes—a move that was approved by the full legislature without a blink. It took a while for the repercussions to be recognized in Mississippi's courtrooms. Women were now a part of the jury venire.

Jewell described the courthouse bathroom visit as well as the trip out of town during the trial lunch break. She also described the harrowing departure from Macon after the verdict, complete with red lights. She had a very clear memory of the efforts by the owners of the Red Hot Truck Stop to graciously accommodate black diners, against the grain of the times.

I believed the role of the political climate of the forties, fifties, and sixties was crucial to creating a brooding atmosphere for the story. It was important, I thought, to provide as many campaign and political details as possible so that readers would understand the blatancy of the racism that pervaded the decades. It appeared to me that unchecked racism constituted a constant threat to the McMahans and Gastons. I felt it was important to describe the cultural wars that were underway during the summer they were waiting for the appeal, when Mississippi was sweltering under a record heat wave. The election season of 1959 was one of the most racially charged shows in the country, and the Gaston and McMahan families were in danger for fighting the white establishment. It was serious enough to require a highway patrol escort out of town after the trial. As one who lived in Mississippi during the era of the civil rights movement, just putting language to the climate we struggled under was a catharsis. I encountered still raw emotions in my sources and myself during the writing of this book.

It was also during this time period that W. L. Griffin burst the comfort bubble of Hattiesburg with the revelations of *Black Like Me*. Jewell spoke first of Bryce's outreach to P. D. East related to the publication. Mike revealed that his father's contributions to the NAACP were confirmed by family employee Willie Ruth.

Eventually, thanks to the Citizens "Clan," revenue dried up for the *Petal Paper*. Though East hung on for a while after the 1960 Griffin embroilment, he finally closed shop and moved.

As it turned out, Theron Lynd won the circuit clerk's seat and proved to be extremely successful at his charge to keep blacks from voting, so much so that he drew the Justice Department's attention before he'd been in office a year and was a defendant in a protracted federal legal battle for much of the sixties due to his role in inhibiting the African American vote in Forrest County.

The progeny of the White Citizens' Council organization is said to be the modern-day Council of Conservative Citizens, headquartered in St. Louis, Missouri. At one point, Mississippi's contemporary legislature boasted thirty-four members of the Council of Conservative Citizens.

In 2008, House Bill No. 207 Reg. Sess. resoundingly passed both chambers of the Mississippi legislature, posthumously dedicating a stretch of Beach Boulevard in Biloxi as Dr. Gilbert R. Mason Sr. Memorial Highway.

Jewell provided the details and narrative surrounding the subterfuge that eventually led to the end of the *State v. Gaston* cases. She was careful to conceal the true identities of her gentlemen helpers. Ella's daughters burst with laughter, Mike reported, when they learned why their mother would suddenly get sick on Sundays and Mrs. Mac would show up to take her to the hospital. Mike described one of the most vivid memories of his life, the trek across Highway 49 to Forrest General Hospital. He helped me flesh out the circumstances of the day, stating that he actually heard his mother yelling down the hall as he left the hospital, and introducing me to coconspirator Esta at his mother's birthday party in 2012. She confirmed the tale of the red rubber hot-water bottles.

Nearly all dialogue not found in the court documents or newspaper accounts are from statements told to me by sources during our interviews. And, some I created to move the plot along or to develop the characters.

I have observed that lawyers who defend the State of Mississippi's statutes and lower court decisions are not always philosophically aligned with their charge. Attorneys are trained to set their personal ideas aside as best they can and rely solely on the letter of the law in exercising their professional duties. So, while Assistant Attorney General Lyell may have compiled an impressive record in maintaining the "legal" separation of the races, I cannot in good conscience assign unkind motives to his acts. When we lost Governor Bill Allain in late 2013, many people commented on his successful representation of the state in many such actions, but that once elected to public office, he forcefully used the power of his positions to make sure that minorities and women had equal and honored opportunities to succeed in Mississippi.

I was never able to identify a couple of people—Nelse Gaston's employer who, like the McMahans, had been a stalwart supporter of his friend and employee throughout the ordeal, according to Jewell. I named him Bill Johnson after my own stalwart supporter. I also changed the name of a Noxubee County resident who is alleged to have committed the cold-blooded murder over a travel right-of-way dispute. Although the alleged perpetrator was mentioned by name to me on several occasions during local interviews, he was never convicted in a court of law. As they say in America, we are innocent until we are proven guilty.

SELECTED
RESOURCES

Much of this book is based on interviews and conversations with Jewell McMahan, Voncile Gaston Burkett, Jean Gaston Hill, Mike McMahan, Mayor Velma Hill Jenkins, Mayor Bob Boykin, Ike Brown, Willie Ruth Twilley Jones, Charlie Watkins, Representative Reecy Dickson, Gaston cousin John Lewis, Mrs. Harpole Patterson, Attorney John Christopher, newspaper publisher Scott Boyd, and Noxubee County Circuit Clerk Carl Mickens.

Although not an exhaustive list, the following resources were also instrumental in the writing of this book.

Alston, Alex A. Jr., and James L. Dickerson. *Devil's Sanctuary: An Eyewitness History of Mississippi Hate Crimes*. Chicago: Lawrence Hill Books, 2009.

Blackwell, Unita. *Barefootin': Life Lessons from the Road to Freedom*. New York: Crown Publishers, 2006.

Boyd, Scott, publisher. Various articles. *The Macon Beacon*. Nineteenth and twentieth centuries.

Ella Gaston v. State of Mississippi. No. 41617 (Supreme Court, State of Mississippi, September 3, 1960).

Gannett Publishing, Inc. Various articles. *The Clarion-Ledger.* Twentieth century.

_____. *The Hattiesburg American.* Twentieth century.

Griffin, John Howard. *Black Like Me.* New York: New American Library, 1960.

Henry, Aaron. *Aaron Henry: The Fire Ever Burning.* Jackson, MS: The University Press of Mississippi, 2000.

Johnston, Erle. *I Rolled with Ross!* Baton Rouge, LA: Moran Publishing, 1980.

_____. *Mississippi's Defiant Years 1953-1973.* Forest, MS: Lake Harbor Publishers, 1990.

_____. *Politics: Mississippi Style.* Forest, MS: Lake Harbor Publishers, 1993.

Katagiri, Yashuhiro. *The Mississippi State Sovereignty Commission: Civil Rights and States' Rights.* Jackson: The University Press of Mississippi, 2001.

Lemann, Nicholas. *Redemption: The Last Battle of the Civil War.* New York: Farrar, Straus and Giroux, 2006.

Martin, Gordon A. Jr. *Count Them One by One: Black Mississippians Fighting for the Right to Vote.* Jackson: The University Press of Mississippi, 2010.

Mississippi State Sovereignty Commission. "Mississippi Department of Archives and History, Sovereignty Commission Online." www.mdha.state.ms.us. 2010-2012.

Nash, Jere, and Andy Taggert. *Mississippi Politics: The Struggle for Power, 1976-2006.* Jackson: The University Press of Mississippi, 2006.

Ratliff v. Beale. Mississippi State Supreme Court opinion. 1896.

Smith, Timothy B. "Jackson: The Capital City and the Civil War." mississippihistorynow.mdah.state.ms.us. April 2010.

The State of Mississippi v. Ella Gaston. No. 3644 (Noxubee County Circuit Court, February Term 1960).

Staten, Charles. "Bull Deale's Beheading." *Mississippi Oral History Project: Noxubee County Library.* Oral History (Macon, Mississippi, August 7, 2009).

United States of America, Plaintiff Appellant. v. Emmett W. Farrar et al., Defendants-Appelees. No. 27125 (United States Court of Appeals Fifth Circuit, August 14, 1969).

United States Congress. *Volume 11.* Report of and Testimony, Congress Joint Select Committee on the Condition of Affairs in the Late Insurrectionary States. 1872.

Watson, Bruce. *Freedom Summer: The Savage Season That Made Mississippi Burn and Made America a Democracy.* London: Viking Penguin, 2010.

Williams, Ann. *In the Cold Light of Day.* Jackson, MS: LeFleur's Bluff Publications, Inc., 1998.

APPENDIX – THE DECISION

Supreme Court Decision
Ella Gaston v State of Mississippi

Writing for the Court: ETHERIDGE, Justice

Appellant, Ella Gaston, was convicted in the Circuit Court of Noxubee County of a misdemeanor, attempting to obstruct an officer in the performance of his duties. She had previously been convicted in a justice of the peace court, and had appealed. The pertinent statute, Miss. Code 1942, Rec., Sec. 2294, provides: If any person or persons by threats or force, abuse or otherwise, attempt to intimidate or impede a judge, justice of the peace, juror, witness, prosecuting or defense attorneys or any officer in the discharge of his duties or to obstruct or impede the administration of justice in any court, he shall, upon conviction, be punished by imprisonment in the county jail, not less than one month, nor more than six months and by fine not exceeding three hundred dollars. Appellant and her husband, who are Negroes, live in Hattiesburg, Mississippi. On February 22, 1959 they and six of their grandchildren drove about one hundred and forty miles to Shuqualak to visit relatives. The incident for which appellant was convicted occurred that afternoon, as she and her husband were preparing to return to

Hattiesburg. Nelse is appellants husband, and the affidavit charged her with attempting to intimidate or impede the sheriff in arresting him for the crime of driving a car while under the influence of intoxicating liquor. E. W. Farrar, sheriff at the time, was one of the principal witnesses for the state. On direct examination he was asked where he first saw Nelse Gaston that day. The sheriff replied: We were investigating and trying to find a Negro by the name of Frank Ed Hill, that had committed an assault upon the marshal down there (Shuqualak). Appellants counsel objected, on the ground the statement was irrelevant and inflammatory. The objection was overruled. This was reversible error. What happened in Shuqualak the night before, when appellant and her husband were in Hattiesburg, was wholly irrelevant to an issue pertaining to her guilt or innocence. It unnecessarily raised in the trial the element of racial prejudice, which has no place in the administration of justice. Hardaway v. State, 99 Miss. 223, 54 So. 833 (1911); Reed v. State, 232 Miss. 432, 99 So. 2d 455 (1958). The jury had the duty and right to evaluate the testimony independently of that emotional factor being injected into the case by the states counsel and witnesses. Moreover, two other events during the trial presented this same factor to the jury. Deputy Sheriff Hutcherson testified to the same effect, defendants objection was sustained, but the court overruled the motion of appellants counsel to direct the jury to disregard it. In addition, the opening argument of states counsel to the jury told it the same thing, and also that defendants husband was related to the party for whom the officers were searching, although there is no evidence to that effect. The trial court sustained an objection to the opening argument, and instructed the jury to disregard the remarks. Subsequently, the sheriff testified as described above, and the court overruled appellants objection. Deputy Sheriff Hutcherson testified further that the officers searched the car occupied by appellant, and belonging to her husband, and found a .22 caliber rifle under the seat. Objection of appellants counsel was overruled, although the trial court stated it had been very liberal in letting in a lot of incompetent proof. Appellant was being tried on a charge of attempting to impede or intimidate the sheriff in arresting her husband. There was no evidence that she or her husband were attempting to remove or use the rifle, or that she owned it. The fact that the officers found it in the husbands car was wholly irrelevant to the issues made in the affidavit, and had a tendency to further unduly prejudice the jury. It was error to overrule appellants objection to that testimony.

After omitting the formal parts, the affidavit charges that Ella Gaston did willfully and unlawfully attempt to impede and intimidate Emmett W. Farrar, the duly qualified and acting Sheriff of Noxubee County, Mississippi, in the discharge of the duty of said Emmett W. Farrar as such Sheriff, by approaching said Sheriff with a womans handbag containing a pistol and opening said bag and stating to the said Sheriff 'you can not arrest my husband, when he the said Sheriff was legally arresting one, Nelse Gaston, husband of said Ella Gaston for the crime of driving an automobile while under the influence of intoxicating liquor against the peace and dignity of the State of Mississippi.

The offense defined by Code Sec. 2294 requires the state to show (1) an attempt to intimidate or impede an officer in the discharge of his duties, (2) by threats or force, abuse or otherwise. Defendants demurrer to the sufficiency of the affidavit was overruled. This was error. The charge is an attempt to impede and intimidate the sheriff, by approaching him with a pistol in defendants handbag, opening it, and saying you cannot arrest my husband. This does not constitute threats or force or abuse. It does not charge or indicate a present intent to attempt to impede the sheriff. The phrase or otherwise refers to acts or stratagem of the same general nature as the preceding threats, force or abuse. An attempt, represented by an overt act, is not sufficiently charged under the statute. Wilson v. State, 80 Miss. 388, 31 So. 787 (1902); 39 Am. Jur., obstructing Justice, Secs. 8-11; Anno., 48 A.L.R. 746 (1927).

Merely remonstrating with an officer in behalf of another, or criticizing an officer while he is performing his duty, does not amount to an attempt to intimidate or impede him. 3 Anderson, Whartons Criminal Law and Procedure (1957), Sec. 284. On the key issue in this case, the affidavit fails to charge that appellant approached the sheriff, stating he could not arrest her husband, because he had done nothing, opened her bag containing a pistol and reached in it. The insufficient charge of an overt act rendered the affidavit demurrable. Also, there is a variance between the affidavit and the proof: The officers arrested appellants husband for reckless driving, not driving while under the influence, as the affidavit charges.

Finally, there is such a material disparity between the testimony of the states principal witnesses in the justice of the peace court, at which a transcript of their testimony was also taken, and that in the circuit court, that we are of the opinion that justice would be better promoted by a new trial of this case before another jury. This is particularly so in view of the prejudicial testimony, described above, which was admitted in evidence. Cole v. State, 217 Miss. 779, 65 So. 2d 262 (1953); Jefferson v. State, 52 So. 2d 925 (Miss. 1951); Dickerson v. State, 54 So. 2d 925 (Miss. 1951). There is no direct proof that appellant intended to use the pistol that was in her handbag, and, in view of the disparity in the proof on the two trials on the key issue of whether she even opened the handbag, some of the judges believe there is not sufficient evidence to sustain a conviction in a criminal case. However, since the case will have to be reversed for the above stated reasons, it is not necessary for us to decide that issue at this time.

Reversed and remanded.

McGEHEE, C. J., and KYLE, ARRINGTON and GILLESPIE, JJ., concur.

239 Miss. 420, 123 So.2d 546

CPSIA information can be obtained
at www.ICGtesting.com
Printed in the USA
FSHW011253030521
81081FS